IN SEARCH OF THE
ORIGINAL KORAN

IN SEARCH OF THE
ORIGINAL KORAN

THE
TRUE HISTORY
OF THE
REVEALED TEXT

MONDHER SFAR

TRANSLATED BY EMILIA LANIER

Prometheus Books

59 John Glenn Drive
Amherst, New York 14228–2119

Published 2008 by Prometheus Books

Inquiries should be addressed to
Prometheus Books
59 John Glenn Drive
Amherst, New York 14228–2119
VOICE: 716–691–0133, ext. 210
FAX: 716–691–0137
WWW.PROMETHEUSBOOKS.COM

12 11 10 09 08   5 4 3 2 1

Library of Congress Cataloging-in-Publication Data

Sfar, Mondher.
    [Coran est-il authentique? English]
    In search of the original koran : the true story of the revealed text / Mondher Sfar.
        p. cm.
    Includes bibliographical references and index.
    ISBN 978–1–59102–521–4
    1. Islam—controversial literature. 2. Koran—Evidences, authority, etc. I. Title.
BP169.S4313 2007
297.1'221—dc22

2007011481

Printed in the United States of America on acid-free paper

CONTENTS

INTRODUCTION   9

CHAPTER 1. THE KORAN IS NOT
            THE ORIGINAL ONE   15

Transmission of Meaning   18
The Theory of Variants   20
The Variants of the Koran   22
From Variation to Manipulation   26
The Satanic Revelations   28
By the Prophet's Side   31
Other Ambiguities of the Mode of Revelation   31
The Whole Revelation?   34
Lost or Unretained Texts   36

Two Brief Prayers Removed from the Koran   39
On Interpolation   40

CHAPTER 2. THE COMPONENTS
OF THE KORAN   49

The Verses: A Late Invention   49
The Surahs   52
The Preambles   54
The Mysterious Letters   57
The Division of Surahs   62
The *Basmala* and *al-Raḥmân*   64
The Titles of Surahs   67

CHAPTER 3. WRITINGS OF THE KORAN   69

The Difficulties of the Writing   75
The Myth of "Uthmân"   78
The Manuscript of Samarkand   79
The Myth of Authenticity   81
The Scribal Function   82
Stereotypes and Phraseology   83
The Practice of Recomposition   84
Al-qur'ân, a Scribal Work   85

CHAPTER 4. MYTHS AND PREJUDICES   87

The Myth of Originality   88
From the *Kitâb* to the *Qur'ân*   90
The Myth of the Collection   94
The Myth of Perfect Transmission   95

The Myth of Inimitability   96
Authenticity of the *Waḥy*   98

CONCLUSION   **101**

APPENDIX: THE SOLAR ECLIPSE
          OF JANUARY 27, 632 CE   **105**

The Sole Scientific Date   105
A Great Enigma   109
A Conjugal Psychodrama   111
The Eclipse and the Farewell Pilgrimage   114

NOTES   **117**

BIBLIOGRAPHY   **125**

INDEX   **135**

INTRODUCTION

Q uestioning the authenticity of the Koranic text these days smacks of blasphemy, of a particularly sacrilegious act with regard to one of the principal dogmas of Islam—if not the most important one, after belief in God and in his Prophet. However, the taboo that envelops the question of the history of the Koran has no theological justification that emanates from the revealed text—nor even a historical rationale, since Muslim Tradition itself relates an imposing mass of information about the very serious problems that have affected transmission of the Koranic text down to our own day.

But the most astonishing aspect of the tense attitude of Muslim orthodoxy is that it contradicts the very doctrine that the Koran itself has formulated about its own authenticity. In effect, far from claiming any textual authenticity at all, the Koran advances a theory of revelation that resolutely refutes such a claim.

This Koranic doctrine explains that the revealed text is merely a secondary product emanating from a primary and authentic text that has been recorded on a celestial tablet kept by God and inaccessible to common mortals. The true Koran is not the one that has been revealed, but the one that has remained in heaven in the hands of God as sole true witness of the revealed text. In short, the Koran attributes authenticity not to the text revealed through Muhammad, but only to the original kept by God. This means that the passage from the heavenly original to the copy betrays the letter of the transmitted text. Muhammad did not receive the revelation by means of dictation, but by means of inspiration (*wahy*).

Moreover, the revealed text was subject to the law of abrogation and to divine editing, in such a way that the Koran is neither eternal nor absolute. It is historical, circumstantial, and relative. Other factors distance it from the authentic heavenly text: God orders Satan to inspire false revelations from the mouth of Muhammad, and then he denounces them. Moreover, the Prophet is subject to certain human weaknesses—again, according to the Koran.

Thus it is important to bring to light this Koranic doctrine about the inauthenticity of the revealed text.

In effect, at the death of the Prophet, the text of the revelation found itself consigned onto several mediums: parchments, scapular bones, shards, and other chance materials. By all the evidence, the idea of gathering these scattered texts into a single compendium was a rather late innovation, unknown to Muhammad and foreign to the spirit of the Koran. Only a shaping of revealed textual units saw the light of day during Muhammad's lifetime. These units of revelation gave rise to the current *surahs* by a process that has still not been elucidated, but which is partially visible through the mysterious letters that open certain chapters.

Muslim Tradition maintains that a first collection of the Koran was carried out by the first caliph, Abû Bakr. A fresh collection was undertaken under the third caliph, Uthmân. What did such a "collection" consist of? In fact, opinions on this subject vary, and nothing certain has come down to us. The situation is all the more obscure in that a third collection is supposed to have taken place during the reign of the Umayyad governor al-Hajjâj.

Whatever these incoherences within Muslim doctrine about the history of the Koranic text, it is clear that the establishment of an official text of the Koran was the end result of a long progression, whose stages can only be deduced approximately and with great prudence on the basis of stories reported in Muslim Tradition.

In short, the first generations of Muslims did not possess the Koranic text of reference, since one had never existed. As consolation, tradition purely and simply created the myth of the archangel Gabriel meeting Muhammad annually for a clarification of the texts revealed in the course of the preceding year. Thus it was that upon the death of the Prophet that the Koranic text found itself entirely codified, structured, and completed according to divine wishes: the "collections" that took place later have brought nothing new, according to certain stories; they have merely rectified the alterations that intervened during the first decades of Islam. This is the mythical orthodox doctrine about the reliability of the transmission of the revealed text.

In parallel with this idealist justification, Muslim Tradition has bequeathed us indications that are very useful for the historian of the Koranic text, on the condition (of course) that one knows how to decode them. It is on the basis of this material that critical study of the Koranic text began in the West through a magisterial book (which remains even today a reference work) by Theodor Nöldeke, *Geschichte des Qorans*, or *The History of the Koran*, published for the first time in 1860, and reissued in 1909 by Friedrich Schwally, an edition continued in 1919 with the second volume and in 1938 by Gotthelf Bergsträsser. It inspired in 1958 the excellent *Introduction au Coran* by the French scholar Régis Blachère.

Alongside this historical critique of the Koran, a new scholarly research avenue arose around the middle of the twentieth century, devoted to the study of the literary genres employed in the sacred text of Islam. Again it was the German school that led the way in this new orientation, essentially inspired by a discipline in which it excelled, that of *Formgeschichte*, of which Rudolf Bultmann (1884–1976) was one of the leading figures. Let me mention the series of articles published in 1950 in the journal *The Muslim World* titled "The Qur'ân as Scripture," which prefigured the important contribution of John Wansbrough in his *Quranic Studies*. Wansbrough studied the schemas of the Koranic discourse and compared them to the Jewish tradition. His demonstration of a solidly structured discourse suggests in effect that it was continuing an old scribal tradition. Henceforth the text of the Koran appears less as the result of an improvisation issuing from the desert than as the continuation of a lofty tradition.

We are going to make use of these scriptural techniques in order to better understand the history of the composition of the Koranic text as realized by the veritable technicians of the inspired writing.

I will end this study by insisting that myths were created by Muslim Tradition in order to impose a representation of the revelation and of its textual product—which, as we shall see, is totally alien to the spirit and to the content of the Koranic text as it has been handed down to us.

Finally, I want to thank all those who have encouraged me to pursue my research and have offered me the benefit of their kind assistance. I particularly appreciate the help of editor Ibn Warraq for this English version, and translator Emilia Lanier for correcting the proofs.

Mondher Sfar

NOTE FROM THE TRANSLATOR

The French translation of quotations from the Koran used by Mr. Sfar refers to the one by Régis Blachère. My English translation also makes use of this, as well as of the standard English versions by Marmaduke Pickthall, the N. J. Dawood translation for Penguin, and that by A. Yusuf Ali. The chapter and verse numbers corresponding to

Koranic quotations are indicated, separated by a colon, between parentheses in the text. Occasional biblical references use the New International Version (NIV) and occasionally the New Revised Standard Version (NRSV).

The system of transliteration adopted in this book aims at simplicity. We have used primarily the English form of proper names and common nouns that are habitually used. As for dates, the Muslim calendar is used (H = Hijra) alongside the Judeo-Christian one (CE = Common Era). Readers who want to pursue the subject are referred to the bibliography and the sources in the notes found at the end of this book.

Emilia Lanier

Chapter 1

THE KORAN IS NOT THE ORIGINAL ONE

Thereafter the transmission of the divine message to Muhammad took place in a particular mode that is more complex than the one represented in orthodox Muslim doctrine. According to the latter, God literally dictated his message. Thus Muhammad is meant to have reproduced in the Koran the words that were created for all eternity by Allah.

In fact, the text revealed to the Prophet comes from another text kept close to God. This is the famous tablet, in Arabic *lawh*, the exclusive property of God, and to which he is the only one to have access, along with the angel-scribes or angel-messengers like Gabriel. It was only on the basis of this original that the Koranic text was transmitted to Muhammad and then to mankind. From the start, then, the Koran establishes a distinction of decisive importance within the process of revelation.

Here in effect lies a question central to our inquiry into the authenticity of the revealed text. Consequently, Koranic doctrine is clear: the revealed Koranic text represents merely a supposed copy that cannot be confused with the heavenly original, and in this sense, it could not possibly pretend to be authentic. Here, the Koranic text is free from ambiguity: the heavenly original is designated by the term *kitâb*, which signifies "writing," while the text that derives from it by means of revelation is called *qur'ân*, an entity that is essentially liturgical and designates recitation.

Between the copy and the original, there is a whole history that quite evidently refers us to the nature of revelation and to the mode of transmission it is presumed to employ. Cleary understood, the decisive question that we would want to pose at the outset is more theological than historical. And we shall see that the Koranic philosophy of the nature of revelation illuminates in an original and unsuspected manner the history of the transmission of the Koran down to our day.

First let me rectify a misunderstanding long maintained by Muslim orthodoxy. In order to prove that the Koranic text is perfectly authentic, it has been alleged that God committed himself to preserving it from any alteration due to the vagaries of its transmission through time and across generations. This doctrine was essentially founded on this verse: "We have, without doubt, sent down the Message (*dhikr*); and We will assuredly guard it (*innâ lahu laḥâfizûn*)" (15:9). One often finds this verse as an epigraph in Koran copies in order to stress their authenticity. Does the *dhikr* refer here to the Koranic text? In fact, study of the occurrences of this term in the Koran show that *dhikr* designates the genre of the tale that one is citing (*dhakara*, i.e., to cite) for pedagogic purposes, in order to draw a lesson from it. The Koran utilizes this term specifically to designate the tales of ancient peoples like 'Âd, *Thamûd*, and so on, which believers are called upon to keep in their memories. God thus possesses the detailed stories of these peoples, which he keeps close to himself. This is repeated elsewhere: the message (*tadhkira*) is found "in Books held in honor, exalted, kept pure and holy, [written] by the hands of scribes honorable and pious and just" (80:13–16). And so it is clear that *dhikr* refers not to the Koranic text but to the ensemble of stories drawn from the heavenly pages, which benefit from the greatest divine care. It is the same for the *qur'ân,* which is still drawn from a heavenly original: "This is a Glorious *Qur'ân* (recitation), [inscribed] in a Tablet Preserved! (*mahfûz*)" (85:21–22). Although here the Arabic text does not tell us clearly whether it is the tablet (the original) or the recitation that is the object of conservation, in any case, this recitation is authenticated by means of the celestial tablet that exists as the original. And like any original, it is the object of every care—"by the hands of scribes honorable and pious and just"—and especially of every kind of vigilance: " . . . in a Book well-guarded, which none shall touch but those who are clean" (56:78–79). Note that at no time are these heavenly guardians occupied with the safekeeping or preservation of the recited copy (*qur'ân*) from any alteration in the course of its transmission across the generations.

In addition, the text revealed to Muhammad constitutes only an extract of the great book (*kitâb*) in God's possession, which includes among other things the chronicle of the world. When Pharaoh challenged Moses by posing this question—"What then is the condition of previous generations?"—the latter replied: "The knowledge of that (*'ilmuhâ*) is with my Lord, duly recorded (*kitâb*) [by means of which] my Lord never errs, nor forgets" (20:51–52). So this is a matter of a veritable celestial library containing the knowledge of the world, from which is extracted the Koranic revelation, as well as the other Abrahamic revelations.[1]

The idea that this heavenly book is consigned to a preserved tablet is quite ancient, going back to the Sumerians.[2] They bequeathed to us the idea of destiny consigned to writing: *maktûb* is an important concept in Oriental and Arab-Muslim mentality, found in the Koran through the expression *kutiba 'alâ:* "[it has been] decreed to [someone]."

Similarly, it is the original of the book—and not its copy—that God has committed himself to preserving, for example, when he orders Muhammad: "And recite what has been revealed to you of the Book (*kitâb*) of thy Lord: none can change His Words (*kalimât*), and you shall find no refuge besides Him" (18:27). Since the original text is not subject to the principle of change, the Prophet could not feel authorized to modify the recited copy. We can indeed see that the original serves as a source of authentication, and at the same time as a dissuasive argument against any attempt at falsehood, including on the part of the Prophet himself.

This original, moreover, is designated as "Mother of the Book" (*umm al-kitâb*): "By the Book that makes things plain [. . .] in the Mother of the Book, in Our Keeping" (43:2–4). This notion of "Mother" signifies in the Arabic language the "source," or else the "center," as in the Koranic expression "the mother of cities" (*umm al-qurä*), referring to Mecca as the Arab capital. It is the very function of the original to play the role of matrix or kernel from which the copy is drawn. Thus we see appearing a genetic relation, or rather the *precedence* of an immutable original over a copy exposed to all dangers.

However, another term exists that is utilized in the Koran to refer to the troubled relation between the original and the copy, the verb *ṣaddaqa*, as in this passage from the Koran: "That which We have revealed to you of the Book (*kitâb*) is the Truth, in accordance (*muṣaddiqan*) with [the original Book] that is in His possession (*mâ bayna yadayhi*)" (35:31). The revelation is here declared through the verb *ṣaddaqa*, meaning conforming or faithful to the heavenly original.

TRANSMISSION OF MEANING

But does this mean that this conformity signifies a literal identity between the copy and its original? Here the answer can only be negative, since this notion of conformity is applied in the Koran to designate the type of relationship between previous revealed texts that necessarily differ among themselves in the letter, but are identical as to their spiritual content: "now that a Book [the Koran] confirming (*muṣaddiq*) their own has come to them [Jews] from God . . ." (2:89). Just as the "Gospel" coming through Jesus conforms to the Torah (5:46), so the book (*kitâb*) coming through Muhammad conforms to the "Scripture" (5:48). These examples demonstrate that the conformity of the copy to its original is identical to that which exists between the revealed texts. The copy revealed to Muhammad is thus far from reproducing literally the heavenly text (*kitâb*) consigned to the tablet guarded by the pure angels: according to the Koran, it merely conserves its general meaning.

For their part, Muslim traditionalists have not hesitated to formulate clearly hypotheses about the literal nonconformity between the heavenly original and its copy transmitted by Muhammad. Thus, Suyûtî (died in 1505 CE)—author of a treatise that remains a model of its kind on the Koran—lays out three hypotheses about the mode of transmission of the original text. The first is quite evidently that of the literal conformity between the original and the copy. The second hypothesizes that the archangel "Gabriel could have descended especially [*sic*] with the meanings [of the Koran], and Muhammad could then have learned these meanings and expressed them in the language of the Arabs." The third hypothesis is that "Gabriel would have received these meanings [of the Koranic text] and he would have expressed them in the Arabic language—the inhabitants of Heaven would have read the Koran in Arabic—and in this way he would have made it descend [onto Muhammad]."[3] Here we see that the last two hypotheses clearly advance the idea of the literal inauthenticity of the Koranic text with respect to the heavenly original.

One verse of the Koran even chimes with the second scenario of the transmission of the heavenly text: "We have made it [the *kitâb*] a recitation (*qur'ân*) in Arabic" (43:3). So it is indeed God and his angelic scribes, with Gabriel at their head, who are thought to have proceeded to the elaboration of the Arabic text received by Muhammad. Still, one should not necessarily see this Arabic version as a literal translation of the original. Tradition even claims that Gabriel had not himself read the heavenly tablet and that God, in order to transmit his words, had inspired in him "[the] revealed [Words] (*takallama bi-al-wahy*)." This divine inspiration in a loud voice is said to "make Heaven tremble for fear of God. And as soon as the inhabitants of Heaven hear [these words], they are struck by lightning and fall down prostrate. And the first who lifts his head is Gabriel. This is when God communicates to him orally what He wants of His revelation. Gabriel dictates in his turn these Words to [other angels]. And in each one of the Heavens, the inhabitants ask him: 'What did our Lord say?' and Gabriel replies: '[He said] the Truth.'" And this is how Gabriel transmits the revelation from heaven to heaven down to Muhammad, his final recipient.[4]

The exegete Al-Juwaynî has split things down the middle. For him, the Koran contains two genres of juxtaposed texts that conform to two customary possibilities of transmission of missives within royal tradition. One part of the Koranic text is said to be transmitted according to the meaning, without taking into account the letter of the original text dictated by God. The other part, inversely, is said to be a copy literally conforming to the message dictated by God.[5]

THE THEORY OF VARIANTS

With this doctrine of a revelation transmitted according to the meaning and not according to the letter, we attain a new stage in the rupture of the unity of the Koranic revelation. After having witnessed the splitting of the revelation into an original and a copy, and then the literal differentiation between the two, we now arrive at the explosion of the copy into a multiplicity of possibilities of literal expression. This is the theory advanced by the Tradition of the Seven Letters (*sabᶜ ahruf*), or Seven Readings (*sabᶜ qirâ'ât*). Tradition justifies this theory by means of a *hadîth* reported by Uthmân, which has Muhammad say: "The Koran descended according to Seven Letters."[6]

Suyûtî asserts that this *hadîth* has been interpreted in forty ways. Among them, Ibn Qutayba's thesis explains that it must have been a matter of seven "modes of variation" of the Koran's text, as follows: 1) that of declension, without the meaning being affected; 2) that of verb tenses; 3) that of letters with the same graphic form but having different diacritical signs; 4) that of letters similar in their graphics; 5) that of the place of groups of words in the sentence; 6) variation of the text by adding or suppressing words; and finally, 7) variation in words according to their synonyms.[7] Al-Râzî, for his part, adds variations of words of the Koran by the kind, number, and mode of pronunciation.[8] The same Suyûtî relates a thesis, reported by Ibn Hanbal, explaining the "Seven Letters" as the possibility for each word of the Koran to be replaced by seven synonyms.[9] Ubayy, one of the secretaries of Muhammad charged with the redaction of the Koran, was even said to have expressed this as a rule that he applied in his version of the Koran: "I said [in the Koran] Magisterial and Learned, [instead of] Powerful and Wise, [but without going so far as to betray the meaning, as is done when] one substitutes the expression for pardon with one for punishment, or vice versa."[10] Thus, Ubayy, one of the most important scribes of the Prophet, whose name is associated with the redaction of the Koran, goes well beyond simple synonymy in establishing the legitimacy of the infinite freedom of variants—on the sole condition, however, that this does not lead to misinterpretation. It has even been said that the second caliph, Umar (to whom has been attributed the first collection of the texts comprising the Koran), made this assertion: "Everything that is said in the Koran is correct (*ṣawâb*) as long as one does not substitute *punishment* for *pardon* (i.e., one does not commit misinterpretation)."[11]

Suyûtî reports here variants used by Ubayy in verse 2:20, substituting for "walk" the synonyms "pass" and "go." Suyûtî also cites variants by Ibn Masʿûd, another secretary to Muhammad, replacing in verse 57:13 the verb "to be patient" with "to wait" and "to delay the outcome."[12] And Suyûtî reports this anecdote: "Ibn Masʿûd asked a reader to read the phrase 'the tree of Zaqqûm shall be the food of the sinner' (44:43–44). But this reader could only pronounce 'the food of the orphan.' Ibn Mas'ûd had him take it again but with no success. So then he asked him: 'Can you pronounce "food of the depraved"?' The man replied 'Yes,' so Ibn Mas'ûd told him: 'Then keep this expression!'"[13]

THE VARIANTS OF THE KORAN

Ibn Mujâhid (245–324 CE) explains in his *Book on the Seven Readings* (*Kitâb al-sab'a fî al qira'ât*) that "people were in disagreement about the reading [of the Koran], in the same way they were about the Law. The details (*âthâr*) on the Koran that they derived from the sayings of the Companions of the Prophet and from their Followers contained divergences that are a gracious gift for Muslims."[14] Orthodox writers, faced with the variability of the Koranic text and the consequent danger that hovers over its authenticity, could only be brave in the face of this bad luck. They quite simply transformed inconvenience into an advantage: variability, a source of suspicion, became a divine blessing for a humanity that was linguistically diverse, that found it hard to be content with a rigid literalness. It is this pointless justification of the variants of the Koranic text that has permitted their official adoption and their partial conservation down to our day.

Thus the old companion of the Prophet Anas ibn Mâlik (died in 709 CE) was not embarrassed, according to the chronicler Tabari (died in 923 CE), to substitute for verse 73:6 the verb *aswabu* (to be more just) for the one retained in the official version *aqwamu* (to be more correct).[15] Another type of variant is the inversion of terms, of which one finds an example in the corpus of Ibn Mas'ûd in verse 112:3: "He was not begotten and He has not begotten," instead of "He has not begotten and he was not begotten."[16] Even the most important surah of the Koran, the *Fâtiha* ("The Opening," "Exordium"), has not escaped this uncertainty. Thus, in the verse (1:6), the spelling of the word *sirât* (path) varies, according to Ibn Mujâhid, among the codices, from *sirât* to *zirât*, and he concludes on a note of resignation, " . . . and the *Kitâb* does not specify the spelling."[17] Of course by *"Kitâb,"* the writer means the Koran, undoubtedly such as was reported in the various manuscripts of that epoch. This remark by such an important author is of the greatest interest, since it testifies to the facts that during the first century of Islam there did not as yet exist a written text unified as to its written form, and that the greatest scholars versed in knowledge of the Koranic text found it impossible to decide among the variants offered to them, so much did oral tradition show its modest limitations.

The same opening surah offers us another remarkable variant of the same verse we have just mentioned. While the official vulgate commences this verse with "Take us!" Ibn Mas'ûd substitutes "Lead us!" and in the corpus of Ubayy and Alî this becomes "Guide us! Strengthen us!"; but an anonymous variant gives "May your hand guide us! Take us!"[18]

We find the same thing in the celebrated surah *Al-Asr*: there are important divergences between the official version and those attributed to Ibn Mas'ûd and Alî. In the vulgate we read "By the Hour of the afternoon (*wal-'asri*)! Man is in perdition. Except those who have believed" (103:1–3); yet in the version attributed to Ibn Mas'ûd, we have "By the Hour of the afternoon! Certainly We have created Man for his perdition. Except those who have believed," and in the one attributed to Alî we have "By the Hour of the afternoon! By the vicissitudes of fate! Man is in perdition, and is so until the end of time."[19]

Could this last version, cruelly pessimistic, be an original version, or more precisely a remnant from a first draft that was later ameliorated in both content and form? It is difficult to answer this, of course, given the extreme poverty of ancient sources available to the historian. But we will need to recall this phenomenon, for as we have seen, revelation accommodated—and very liberally—many variations in its literal expression. And textual practice obeyed a continual reworking of its formal shape, which generally passed for a normal exercise. During a walk with Umar, after a dinner given by Abû Bakr, Muhammad heard a man in prayer reciting the Koran in quite a peculiar fashion: "'Who advised him,' the Prophet asked Umar, 'to read the Koran in its first form (*ra_tb*), as it came down? He should read it according to the reading of Ibn Umm 'Abd'!"[20]

This anecdote is of the greatest interest, since it clearly establishes the existence in Muhammad's time of two states of the revealed text: a first state and a reworked state that have been modified and corrected. The form of the freshly revealed text is designated here by *ra_tb,* generally applied to describe edible dates that are freshly picked or that are tender. So, during its revelation, the divine text was destined to undergo a shaping that affected the style as well as the content. This is the case with the variants that we have just seen in the brief surah 103. It is quite probable that the last pessimistic version of this surah constitutes its *ra_tb* form, its primitive state that was destined to be modified.

We may also give another illustration of this process of reworking the text. In the course of his inventory of the Korans in rolls conserved in Istanbul, Solange Ory has found in the second fragment of roll no. 8 (Istanbul nos. 3–4) this variant of verse (10:82): "*fa-ghalabû hunâ al-haqqa* [they here vanquished the Truth]," whereas the Koranic text of the vulgate says "*wa yu_hiqqu al-llâhu al-haqqa* [and God will re-establish the Truth]."[21] The theme of this verse refers to the story of Moses and Pharaoh. When the Egyptian magicians show Moses what they are capable of, he challenges them by neutralizing their charms. It is clear that the variant relates to the first version of the story, which asserts that it is the magicians who at first have the upper hand over Moses, and consequently over God. This last observation appeared, over time, as rather shocking, and so the passage must then have been remodeled in order to give a more suitable version, that of our vulgate.

This reworking of the *ra_tb* text is found again through the variants of verse 2:237, where the act of love is designated by the verb "touch," while Ibn Mas'ûd's version gives "copulate."[22]

Revisions are concerned with conventions, but also with respectability, for example, by using more literary terms like *'ihn* (101:5) in place of *ṣûf* for dyed wool, or *mu'ṣada* (104:8) in place of *muṭbaqa*.[23]

The verse 33:20 ("They think that the Confederates have not withdrawn, and if the Confederates should come, they would wish they were in the desert among the Bedouins") has the following variant attributed to Ibn Masᶜûd: "They think that the Confederates have withdrawn, and when they discover that the Confederates have not withdrawn, they would sooner be in the desert, among the Bedouins." Another verse, 58:4 ("This is imposed so that you may believe in Allah and in his Apostle. Such are the limits [*ḥudûd*] set by Allah") has a radically different variant that is attributed to Ibn Masᶜûd and Ubayy: "This is imposed on you so that you may know that Allah is near to you when you pray, ready to answer when you implore Him. For disbelievers there is a cruel torment!"

Still more important is this variant attributed to Ubayy: "And when Jesus, son of Mary, says 'O Sons of Israel! I am the Apostle of Allah sent to you and I announce to you a Prophet whose community will be the last community and through whom Allah will put the seal on the Prophets and on the Apostles.' [When Jesus says this], the Sons of Israel said, 'This is evident sorcery.'" The official version of the vulgate, however, gives "And when Jesus son of Mary says 'O Sons of Israel! I am the Apostle of Allah sent to you, declaring truthful what in the Torah came before me and announcing an Apostle who will come after me, whose name shall be Ahmad.' But when Jesus came with Proofs, the Sons of Israel said, 'This is evident sorcery!'"(61:6). It is curious to see that where the official version mentions the name "Ahmad," which is supposed to be that of Muhammad, but without mentioning the "seal" of prophecy, Ubayy's version does the inverse. This latter version might be later than that of the vulgate. As we see, while the object of the accusation of sorcery put into the mouths of the "Sons of Israel" are here the "Proofs" given by Jesus, in Ubayy's version the label applies to the announcement of the forthcoming "seal" of the prophets, which is rather incomprehensible. Moreover, Ubayy's version has a more radical tone, insisting more on the primacy of the new religion. Nevertheless, for these reasons one cannot deduce the factualness of Ubayy's version. It might correspond to a reactualization of a text at a time when the rupture with the People of the Book was consummated.

Let me mention one final variant, attributed to Ibn Mas'ûd: "[He is] a Prophet who communicates to you the Scripture that I made descend on him and which contains the stories about the Prophets whom I had sent before him to each people." The official version is rather different: "[Allah has sent] an apostle who proclaims to you the explicit Signs [âya] of Allah, so that he may lead the faithful who do good works from darkness to the light" (65:11).

FROM VARIATION TO MANIPULATION

If the Koran was inspired unto Muhammad according to its meaning and just as it is in the celestial tablet, then it is perfectly comprehensible why the first Muslim generations, starting with the Prophet himself, were not fussy about the letter of the divine message, as we have just seen. Synonymy and successive improvements to the revealed text were part of the prophetic function, just as they were in the work of scribes assigned to this task.

However, this is no longer permissible when it comes to modifying the content of the message, introducing into it ideas not inspired by Allah, or else cutting thematic developments that conformed to the celestial original.

But here is how God himself allows the modification of his own words and overturns the rule of the conformity and eternity of the transmission of his own message: "No Apostle brings a sign (âya) without the permission of Allah. For each period is a Book [revealed]. Allah blots out (yamhû) or confirms what He pleases, and the source [mother] of the Book (umm al-kitâb) is with Him" (13:38–39).

In this important declaration, we may perceive a major contradiction that undermines the unity, identity, and authenticity of the divine message. On the one hand, we have seen that the guarantee of the Koranic text is founded on the existence of an archetype, of an original jealously guarded by the heavenly sovereign. On the other hand, the political and social life of a community is subject to laws of evolution and to changes in power relations. Each stage and each difficulty necessitates a specific decision. This is the precise meaning of the fundamental expression of social theology that we have just read: "For each period is a Book revealed (*li-kulli 'ajal kitâb*)" (13:38). How can one resolve this conflict between a divine text contained in a tablet closely guarded and preserved from any alteration, and the necessity of adapting to a changeable situation, subject to the law of time periods (*'ajal*), and consequently obliged to modify revealed texts according to the contingencies of the moment? The Koran does not seem to have a satisfactory solution to this dilemma. It confines itself to deploring the bad faith of those who see in these modifications the tangible proof of a prophetic deception: "And if We have substituted one sign (*âya*) for another—and Allah knows best What He reveals [in stages]—they say: 'Thou art but a forger!' But most of them do not understand. Say: the Holy Spirit has brought the revelation [Koran] from thy Lord with Truth, in order to strengthen those who believe, and as a Guide and Glad Tidings to Muslims" (16:101–102). We can measure here the breadth of the problem and its gravity. This text clearly echoes the defections of a number of the Prophet's companions after modifications to the revealed text. The Koran alludes to these changes again in an ultimate explanation of these modifications that is not very reassuring: "None of Our revelations do We abrogate (*nansukhu*) or cause to be forgotten, but We substitute something better or similar: Did you not know that Allah has power over all things?" (2:106). And the Koran attacks those who doubt this: "Would you defy [literally, *question*] your messenger as Moses was defied of old?   He that barters faith for ingratitude (*kufr*) has gone astray from the right path" (2:108).

So we see that the Koran's answer to the objections of the Prophet's skeptical entourage can be summed up in an affirmation of divine omnipotence, and that, in every case, the ultimate goal of these changes made to the revealed text was to test the faith of believers. Curiously, the essential rationale for these modifications in the course of revelation was formulated, in a surreptitious manner, as we saw above in verse 13:38, and it was never taken up again or more amply developed. However, advancing an argument about the necessity of adapting to a shifting situation and to problems that arise over time has a major pitfall: it imperils the validity and identity of revelation, even if its divine authenticity remains unquestioned. This dilemma has hung in all its heavy weight over the propagation of the Muslim faith and over the formation of orthodox theology, but also over the elaboration of the canon of Muhammadian revelation. We will come back to this.

THE SATANIC REVELATIONS

If the modifications of the Koran made in the course of revelation—in the name either of the evolution of things or of divine omnipotence—aroused a hostile reaction among the Prophet's immediate entourage, what happens if this is compounded by revelations aroused by Satan—which, moreover, were ordered by God himself? This additional complication in the identity of the Koran has been produced and clearly acknowledged: "And We have assigned for every prophet an enemy: the devils of humankind and Djinns, who inspire each other with vain and varnished falsehoods. If Allah had willed it, they would not have done it" (6:112). These devils (*shayâṭîn*) of human or infernal nature have the function of inducing the Prophet into error. They even go so far as to inspire false revelations in him: "Never did We send a single Messenger or Prophet before you, but when he recited, Satan threw some [false revelations] into his recitation" (22:52). Does the Koran here correspond to the Bible, where in Ezekiel it is a matter of "foolish prophets who follow their own spirit" and whose "visions are false and their divinations a lie. They say 'The Lord declares,' when the Lord has not sent them" (Ezekiel 13:3, 6)? Perhaps. But this is a case of false prophets who are not inspired by God. On the other hand, the Bible does give an example of prophets mandated by God to speak false prophecies. In a vision that the prophet Micaiah had, God asked his angels to help him entice Ahab, king of Israel. One of them then came forward and "stood before the Lord and said, 'I will entice him.' 'By what means?' the Lord asked. 'I will go out and be a lying spirit in the mouths of all these prophets' he said. 'You will succeed in enticing him,' said the Lord. 'Go and do it'" (1 Kings 22:21–22). Thus when the Koran formulates the rule of the test of falsehood that God imposes on all his prophets, it is inscribed within an ancient tradition, of which the Bible offers us here a remarkable illustration.

Let us now envisage the consequences of such a practice upon the revealed texts. For in these conditions of booby-trapped revelations, how can one distinguish the true from the false? The Koran's answer in the verses quoted above is rather reassuring: "Never did We send a single Messenger or Prophet before you, but when he recited, Satan threw some [false revelations] into his recitation. But Allah will cancel (*yansukhu*) anything that Satan throws in and Allah will confirm (*yuhkimu*) His signs. [God does this] to make Satan's interjections a temptation for those whose hearts are tainted, whose hearts are hardened" (22:52–53). We can see that these satanic revelations are diffused among believers like the rest of the divine message, so that the bad ones fall into the trap set for them, and their sins are thereby all the more aggravated. But once this goal is attained, God proceeds to the elimination of the demonic words that he had inspired. But, how? God does not specify.

We are making our way to the emergence of two types of divine revelations: some are true and sure, others are false and doubtful: "It is He who has sent down to you the Book [*kitâb*], wherein are clear revelations (*muhkam*) which are the essential part of the *kitâb* (*hunna ummu al-kitâb*); and other [signs] which are ambiguous (*mutashâbihât*). Those whose hearts are doubtful pursue the ambiguous part, seeking to create dissension (*fitna*) by interpreting it. [But] God alone knows its interpretation" (3:7).

Here we may see clearly the similarity (in the three cases that we have just reviewed) among the three kinds of division that have been introduced into the revealed text: 1) that of the modification of the text; 2) that of satanic revelations; and finally 3) that of the ambiguous nature of a portion of the revelation. In the first case, we are in the presence of suppressed revelations, those contrary to the ones that are "fixed (*thabbata*)" and that conform to the "heavenly tablet (*umm al-kitâb*)" (13:39). But in the third case, the unambiguous text is described as both fixed (*muḥkam*) and as representing "the essential part of the *kitâb* (*umm al-kitâb*)" (3:7); the latter term has been used in the case of textual modification, even though here it does not have quite the same meaning. Similarly, on the subject of the satanic revelations, the healthy part of the revelation is called "clear/confirmed (*muhkama*)"—literally, "fixed," a word used, as we have just seen, to describe the univocal text.

We may conclude from these comparisons that God gives himself the right to suppress a portion of the revealed words, either to improve the text or because these words were dictated by Satan. On the other hand, the equivocal parts (*mutashâbihât*) are treated in a strangely similar way to the suppressed parts, as if they were a revelation of inferior quality, destined to occupy a marginal place. As for the verse 13:39 that we have quoted, God concludes his statement on his capacity to suppress what he wants of revelation with the words: "With Him is the Mother of the Book." This reminder rings as an invitation to consider as doomed to disappear that which does not correspond to this hard kernel of revelation. And so those revelations called *mutashâbihât* have the same status as that part to be suppressed. Moreover, Muslim legal scholars were not mistaken about this when they assimilated these ambiguous revelations to the abrogated verses. But that is another subject.

BY THE PROPHET'S SIDE

The Koran gives us on several occasions the image of a prophet subject to severe pressure from his pagan entourage, Jewish or Christian, pushing him to produce false revelations: "In truth, the [Enemies] sought to entice you from Our Revelations, hoping that you might invent some other scripture against Us, and thus become their trusted friend. And if We had not strengthened your faith, you might have made some compromise with them. In that case, We should have made you taste a double punishment in this life and in death. Then you would have found no ally against Us" (17:73–75).

Moreover, Muhammad hesitates to communicate a part of the revelation: "Perhaps you omit a part of what is revealed to you and you therefore feel anguish . . ." (11:12). Then God orders him to communicate the withheld revelation: "O Messenger! Proclaim what has been sent to you from your Lord. And if you do not, you will have failed to proclaim His message" (5:67). The enemies in effect try by any means to push the Prophet to manipulate the revelation: "Bring us a Reading other than this, or change it." And God makes his Prophet answer them: "It is not for me to change it of my own accord; I follow only what has been revealed to me" (10:15). These same enemies go so far as to pretend to prophesy, with one saying: "'This was revealed to me,' when nothing was revealed to him, or the man who says: 'I can reveal the like of what Allah has revealed'" (6:93).

In the face of this pressure and these provocations, the Prophet attempts to resist, with the help of Allah. Does he succeed? Unfortunately, not always. The satanic revelations, inspired by Allah, are there to illustrate the difficulty of the task.

OTHER AMBIGUITIES OF THE MODE OF REVELATION

Here we touch upon another type of breakdown susceptible to affecting the revealed text, again according to the divine doctrine of the Koran. In the first place there is the technical weakness in the transmission of the revelation by Muhammad. Allah explains to him the right way to communicate: "You need not move your tongue too fast in pronouncing [the revelation]! It is up to Us to see to its collection and recital! When We recite it, follow closely its recitation, and then it is for Us to explain its meaning" (75:16–19).

Another obstacle derives from the Prophet himself: forgetting. Tradition reports a famous story from his wife Aïsha: "The Prophet, having heard someone recite the Koran in the Mosque, said: 'Allah will have mercy on this man, for he has reminded me of some such verse that had escaped me in such-and-such surah.'"[24] Another version relates: "He reminded me of a verse that I had forgotten."[25] The Koran confirms this possibility of forgetting on the part of the Prophet: "None of Our revelations do We abrogate [nansukhu] or cause to be forgotten . . ." (2:106). This forgetting is interpreted here as coming from Allah and being decided upon by Him.

Another characteristic of revelation that makes it an improvised phenomenon, and consequently barely compatible with a preestablished textual project, is its causal link to events in, and the daily history of, the new community created around its prophet. This is what Tradition refers to as "asbâb al-nuzûl," or "that which caused the revealed words."

Even more surprisingly, this Tradition went so far as to make certain of the Prophet's companions veritable "inspirators" of the revealed texts. Suyûtî, for example, devotes chapter 10 of his book Itqân to this phenomenon: "On what was revealed in the Koran according to the expressions pronounced by certain Companions." Suyûtî reports that the companion best illustrated in this domain is the future caliph Umar. His son is supposed to have said: "The Koran recorded nothing literally from what these people say, except for Umar. The Koran was revealed according to certain of his words."[26] Mujâhid is even said to have asserted that sometimes "Umar had a vision and then the Koran was revealed according to that."[27] Several compilers of hadîths have mentioned a saying by Anas that reports:

"Umar said: 'I was in unison with my Lord on three occasions: 1) I said: O Messenger of Allah, if we made the place where Abraham stood a place of prayer?' And then the verse was revealed: 'Make the place where Abraham stood a place of prayer' (2:125); 2) and I said: 'O Messenger of Allah, good people and less good people frequent your women. If you ordered them to veil themselves?' And then the verse of the Veil was revealed; 3) the wives of the Prophet were in league against him because of some story of jealousy and I said to them: 'If perchance the Prophet repudiates you, his Lord will give him wives who are better than you,' and then a verse [66:5] was revealed in these same terms."[28]

Another story, again according to Anas, reports that when this verse is revealed: "We created man from a mass of clay . . ." (23:12), Umar said: "Blessed be Allah, the best of Creators!" and so verse 23:14 was revealed in the same words.[29] Other words of Umar's are said to have been taken verbatim into the Koran, such as: "Whoever is an enemy to Allah and his Angels, and to his Apostles, to Gabriel and Michael, [that one is Allah's enemy] for Allah is an enemy to the unbelievers" (2:98).[30]

Other companions also had the privilege of seeing their words reproduced verbatim in the Koran, as, for example, Sa'd Ibn Mu'âdh, when he exclaimed: "Glory to Thee [our Lord]! This is a most serious slander!" with respect to the accusations circulating against Aïsha, the wife of the Prophet. Thus verse 24:16 textually repeats this exclamation.[31] The same expression has been attributed to others, such as Zayd ibn Hâritha and Abû Ayyûb.[32]

It is also reported that in the course of the battle of Uhud, when Mus'ab ibn 'Umayr was wounded, he did not cease crying: "Muhammad is only a Prophet coming after other Prophets. If he dies or is killed, you will turn back on your heels." Then he died. And so verse 3:144 uses the same words.

In the same lineage of ideas, Suyûtî came to pose a more general question about the historical veracity of words put into the mouths of the angels,[33] and even about the anonymous entourage around God's apostle, as in the prayer of *Fâtiha* (surah 1, "The Opening"): were these words supposed to have been really said by these personages or else only imagined and presumed to have been said?[34] But this question, which relates even more to the semantics and rules of the enunciation, demonstrates the pertinence and the subtlety of the questions posed within Muslim Tradition about the nature of the revealed text, which testifies to an openness of mind and a freedom of inquiry—of which one finds few traces these days.

On the other hand, Tradition tells us of the role of Muhammad's secretaries in the elaboration of certain verses. Zayd ibn Thâbit is said to have asked Muhammad to add two verses, 4:98 and 4:99, in order to exclude the impotent and the blind from the punishment announced in verse 4:97 against those who refused to emigrate from Mecca to Medina and to fight alongside the Prophet.[35]

Even so, there did exist in the circle around the Prophet some dishonest secretaries entrusted with the task of transcribing the revelation. They managed to manipulate the sacred text without Muhammad's knowledge. One of them, who has remained anonymous, had written "the Magisterial, the Clairvoyant" instead of "the Magisterial, the Omniscient," and vice versa. He even made this admission: "I wrote around Muhammad whatever I wanted." Tradition reports that upon his death, each time they tried to bury him, the earth rejected him.[36]

THE WHOLE REVELATION?

One of the principal questions on the subject of the history of the Koran that was raised very early is whether the text that was handed down contains the totality of the divine revelations brought by the Prophet of Islam.

Of course, such a question presupposes from the start two kinds of facts that must be determined before any answer can be given. First, one must wonder about the heavenly tablet from which the revelations are drawn: does it contain a text that is definite in its contours and very precisely determined in its content? There is nothing less certain.

Second, what about the relationship of the copy to its original, also from the standpoint of completeness? Here again, things do not seem very clear, and what we said above on this question enjoins us to the greatest prudence about whether the revealed copy conforms in completeness. When God announces, "This day have I perfected your religion for you" (5:3), it is not a matter of putting a final ending upon a revelation whose termination has never been announced.

But what is most remarkable is the sharp awareness among the first Muslims of the incomplete character of the revelation—starting with Muhammad himself. In fact, during his final pilgrimage to Mecca, he is supposed to have said: "O people! Take [after my example] your legal prescriptions (*ʿilm*) before they are seized [by the angel of death], and before the *ʿilm* rise to Heaven."[37] The Prophet's companions are astonished by this assertion regarding this incompleteness of revelation, since it is supposed to contain the totality of the *ʿilm*. So they ask Muhammad: "O Prophet of Allah! How is it that the *ʿilm* can mount to Heaven when we are in possession of pages (*maṣâḥif*) [of the Koran] . . ." The Prophet, visibly embarrassed, blushes and tells them that the Jews and the Christians, too, have pages but they take no account of them. "In fact, by 'losing the *ʿilm*' one must understand 'the loss of its bearers,'" conclude the authors of the story, somewhat dubiously. Whatever the degree of veracity of this story, it justifies to our intimation of a conviction among the first Muslims—during the Prophet's lifetime and afterward—that the revelation was associated with the destiny of the person of the Prophet, which meant that it would be necessarily broken off at his death. Anas ibn Mâlik is even meant to have said, "God pursued revelation through his Prophet, in the latter's lifetime, until his Prophet had received the majority of what there was of it (*ʿakthara mâ kâna*). And then, [it was only] after this [that] Allah's Apostle died."[38]

From a purely theological standpoint, the Koran has enunciated a principle that definitively denies the idea of completeness of Scripture in the face of the inexhaustible words of God: "Say: If the sea were ink with which to write the words (kalimât) of my Lord, and even if We were to add to it a similar sea to replenish it, the sea would surely run dry before the words of my Lord were spent" (18:109). And, "If all the trees of the earth were pens and the sea, replenished by seven more seas, [were ink], [trees and seas would be exhausted but] the words (kalimât) of God would still not be exhausted" (31:27). Undoubtedly this image belongs to an old tradition, since we find in John, "Jesus did many other things as well. If every one of them were written down, I suppose that even the whole world would not have room for the books that would be written" (John 21:25). The Koran and the Bible are merely drops of water in the face of the ocean of divine words. With this evidence, who could make a claim about the completeness of the Koran—let alone that it could contain the whole science of the universe?

LOST OR UNRETAINED TEXTS

Revelation was conceived as grace, not as a work of art. It could not have an end. Such was the original situation. But from the moment when the idea was born—rather late—of gathering the totality of actually revealed words, it was quickly perceived that this was a totally impossible enterprise. Many texts were forever lost. The son of Caliph Umar could only deplore this fact: "None among you will be able to say, 'I have had the total Koran.' What does he know of its totality! Many [passages] have disappeared from the Koran (qad dha-haba minhu qur'ânun kathîrun). But he should say, 'I had what we know of it.'"[39]

These disappearances are a priori of two kinds. According to the theory of abrogation, which appeared relatively late in Muslim dogma especially along with the emergence of the theory of justice (fiqh), passages of the Koran were abrogated and eliminated from the recitation. But there exists another category of texts lost in the course of the difficult process of transmission of the Koran in the time of

Muhammad and after. It is to this last category that the son of Umar alludes in the astonishing apostrophe that we have just read.

It seems that it is to this same category of lost texts that the theoreticians of the *fiqh* are alluding when they speak of the case of Koranic texts that were abrogated in their recitation and not in their juridical power (*mâ nusikha tilâwatuhu dûna ḥukmuhu*). This is an astonishing case of abrogation! For what reason would God deprive us of legal texts that he intended to maintain in their legislative power? Suyûṭî ventured this justification: the reason was to test the zeal of mankind for obeying divine laws without their having any visible traces; he gave the example of Abraham not hesitating to sacrifice his son as soon as he received the order to do so through a simple vision.[40]

Tradition has bequeathed us numerous testimonies of the loss of revealed texts. For example, Aïsha, the Prophet's wife, is said to have declared: "Surah 33 of the Confederate Tribes (*al-Aḥzâb*) was read in the time of the Prophet with two hundred verses. But when Uthmân wrote the *maṣâḥif* [meaning, fixed the Koranic canon], he was able [to assemble] only what it contains nowadays [that is to say, seventy-three verses]."[41] We note, then, that Caliph Uthmân was unable to find two-thirds of the chapter in question. Other surahs are signaled as having lost an important portion of their initial content. This is the case with surah 24, *al-Nûr* ("The Light"), and of surah 15, *al-Ḥijr*, which are respectively 64 and 99 verses long, as against 100 and 190 originally.[42] Similarly, surah 9, *al-Tawba* ("Repentance"—but initially it bore the name of the incipit, *barâ'a*, or "Innocence") was supposed to have been as long as surah 2, *al-Baqara* ("The Heifer"), that is to say 286 verses, whereas it now has only 129. According to certain chroniclers, this major amputation of more than half the original content would explain why this surah does not contain in its present state the liturgical formula *b'ism 'allâh*, or *basmala*, and why it is in fact the only one without this.[43]

Among the omitted or lost texts, let us mention the celebrated verse on the stoning of the adulterous: "If the old man and old woman fornicate, stone them to death, as a punishment from God, and God is powerful and wise! (*idhâ zanayâ al-shaykhu wa al-shaykha, fa-'rjumûhumâ l-batta nakâlan min Allah, wa Llâhu 'azîzun hakîm*)."[44] In order to certify the authenticity of this verse, tradition reports this speech attributed to Caliph Umar: "God sent Muhammad and revealed the Book to him; and among what he revealed to him there is the verse on stoning. We have recited it, learned and understood it. And God's Messenger has stoned, and we have stoned after him."[45]

There has also been attributed to the same Umar another verse that he was said to have been in the habit of reciting in Muhammad's lifetime: "Do not turn away from the customs of your fathers; this would be impious on your part."[46] And this dialogue is also reported between Umar and a companion on the subject of a misplaced verse: "Umar said to Abd al-Rahmân ibn 'Awf: 'Did you not find among what was revealed to us this verse: "May you fight (*jâhidû*) like you fought the first time!"'? For I could not find it!' And he replied: 'It has disappeared (*usqita*) from the Koran.'"[47]

During the battle of *bi'r ma'ûna*, there was said to have been revealed a verse that puts into the mouths of the dead who fell on this occasion these words that Anas ibn Mâlik, Muhammad's companion, had the habit of reciting as Koranic text: "Make known to those close to us that we have met our Lord who was satisfied with us and who satisfied us." Anas concludes that this verse ended up "returning to Heaven (*hattâ rufi'*)."[48]

Here is another text taken by Tradition as a revelation received by Muhammad: "We have made riches (*al-mâl*) descend [on men] in order that they might make prayers and offer the *zakât* (religious tax). And if the son of Adam had a river [of silver], he would want another one, and if he had two of them, he would want a third. But the belly of the son of Adam will only be filled with earth, and God only pardons he who mends his ways."[49]

Also attributed to Abû Mûsâ al-Ash'arî is a verse from the non-canonic Koran that he is said to have preserved from oblivion: "O you who believe! Do not say that which you do not do, to avoid a testimony being written against you and having to answer for it at the Day of Judgment."[50]

TWO BRIEF PRAYERS
REMOVED FROM THE KORAN

Among the characteristics of the corpus of Ubayy is the presence of two surahs absent from the canon of Uthmân. Apparently they were also included in the corpus of Ibn Abbâs, which has not survived. The first bears the title "The Denial" (al-Khalʿ) and reads as follows: "In the name of Allah, the merciful Benefactor! 1) O, my God, from You we implore aid and pardon! 2) We praise you. We are not unfaithful to you. 3) We renounce and leave those who scandalize you." Ubayy's second noncanonical surah, "The Race" (al-Hafd), runs as follows: "In the name of Allah, the merciful Benefactor! 1) O, my God, it is you we adore. 2) In your honor, we pray and we bow down. 3) Toward you we go running. 4) We await your mercy. 5) We fear your punishment. 6) In truth, Your punishment must strike the Infidels."[51] I concur with Blachère's opinion that these apocryphal surahs are distinguished from the first surah ("The Opening"), "only through some nuances in the language and by the slightly clumsy style." He thinks, too, that they might have been removed from the Uthmân edition due to the fact that they duplicated the Liminary.[52]

It is of the greatest interest to note that whereas Ubayy included in his Koran these two short prayers, as extras to those in the opening Liminary (Fâtiha) and to the two concluding surahs, 113 and 114, on the other hand Ibn Masʿûd rejected in his Koranic rescension not only the two noncanonical surahs, but also the three canonical prayers: 1, 113, and 114. Why such important divergences? Here no doubt we are witnessing the confrontation of two philosophies of the content of the Koranic text: one "rigorous" viewpoint that considers that the prayer is a genre that properly belongs to humankind and that it must be held apart from the divine area, while the viewpoint that we will call "open" or "liberal" considers prayer as an integral part of sacred literature and thereby authorizes its integration into the canon. Let us draw two lessons from this divergence. First, there did not exist in Muhammad's era a very clear vision of the nature of the divine word: Is it a phonetic and literal phenomenon that is strictly codified, or else an authentic inspiration, of course, but one whose literal aspect is of secondary importance? Second, this divergence shows to what extent the contours of the Koranic text were imprecise when the Prophet died, which opened the way to multiple possible canons.

ON INTERPOLATION

Tradition has never concealed the fact that the revealed text underwent interpolations that then passed for authentic passages of the Koran: the archangel Gabriel dictated verses to Muhammad and indicated to him the place where they ought to be inserted—"in this chapter or that." This mythic scenario was conceived to legitimize a posteriori the work of the manifestly arbitrary composition of the Koranic surahs on the basis of those parts of the revealed texts that had a thematic unity. Therefore, most of the surahs of the current Koranic canon are formed of aggregates of revelations, which make them heterogeneous compositions.

This phenomenon inside the surahs is further accentuated by further interpolation within each of the constitutive parts of a surah. In effect, words or phrases may occur inside a thematic development but be distinct from it, either at the level of the composition or at the level of the meaning. Consequently, these interpolations betray a work of textual recomposition of the initial flow and thus constitute so many traces of interventions—divine or human—which are not concerned with being in harmony with the initial text.

The first clue to interpolation is the abnormal proportion taken up by one verse among the other verses in the surah. For example, the verse 2:102 contains thematic developments on the magic used by Solomon and it explains that he cannot be held responsible for it, for instead the fault belongs with the angels Hârut and Mârut, who taught the magic to humans. This argument in favor of Solomon is composed of a single verse that is exceptionally long, eight lines, as opposed to an average of two lines for the surrounding verses. The same is true of this verse: "The angels and the Spirit ascend to Him in the course of one day whose duration is fifty thousand years" (70:4). This is three times longer than the other verses of the same surah and does not have the same rhyme. It is an interpolation that might have been introduced here in the guise of a gloss of the preceding verse, which also mentions the ascent to heaven.

Another category of interpolation consists of the presence of one verse (or more) without a logical link to the idea developed in the text that it interrupts. For example, in the surah "The Heifer," verses 153 to 162 have the theme of encouragements addressed to believers after a military defeat. But in the middle of this development, verse 158 suddenly announces the authorization of the rite of walking around al-Safâ and al-Marwâ, two stations belonging to the pilgrimage route to Mecca. And then the following verses resume the prior thematic development.

Verse 3:92 announces the necessity of almsgiving, without being tied to the preceding theme devoted to the punishments awaiting different categories of infidels.

Verse 5:69 offers a particular case of interpolation, since it repeats word for word verse 2:62. This verse 5:69 was very probably introduced here inadvertently, inasmuch as it expresses a positive appreciation of the "followers of scripture" and other believers, whereas the context in which it is reproduced is marked by recriminations against them.

Another verse without a tie to its context is 5:109. It is caught between two thematic developments—before it, on the testaments of the dying, and after it, on Jesus—while it itself is devoted to prophecy and what is demanded of the prophets on the Day of Judgment.

One also wonders why the brief verse 57:17, devoted to divine omnipotence, has a place in a context devoted to hypocrites.

We may also find a sequence of verses comprising an interpolation in the middle of a development devoted to a different theme. For example, verses 29:18–23 interrupt the story of Abraham to attack those who do not believe in Muhammad and to demonstrate the inevitable character of the punishment that awaits them. And verses 36:69–70 reject the accusation made to the Prophet of being a poet, without any link with the preceding or succeeding verses devoted to the refutation of the belief of Associators. Similarly, verses 55:7–9 introduce the theme of "balance" and the necessity of equity in weights and measures—right in the middle of a thematic development about the omnipotence of God. It is also to be noted that this interpolation is not at the beginning of a new verse but is integrated into the end of verse 55:7.

This kind of interpolation (in the interior of a single verse) is also found in verse 2:189, which contains two different developments: the first devoted to astral phenomena, the second to social graces concerning the manner of entering into homes. Verse 35:18 is composed of two different themes, the first on the principle of individual responsibility, the second on the recipients of divine warnings.

This last figure of interpolation is found again in verse 4:164, where the phrase "Allah spoke directly to Moses" has no link with the beginning of the verse or with the verses that follow. The interpolated phrase is sometimes found in the middle of the verse, as in 6:25 that begins with "Some of them [infidels] listen to you," and suddenly leads to ". . . and we have cast veils over their hearts so they do not understand. We have placed deafness in their ears. If they see every Sign [âya], they do not believe in it." After this interpolation, the text returns to the development broached at the beginning of the verse in these terms: "When they come to you . . ." Another case of faulty interpolation inside a verse: "Indeed we gave the Book to Moses / Be not in doubt that you will meet him / and we made it a guide for the Sons of Israel" (32:23). One clearly sees that this interpolation (placed here between two slashes) can only be a fragment of an unknown development.

Similarly, the interjection "and it was said: 'Away with those who

do wrong!'" placed at the end of verse 11:44, has no link whatsoever
with its beginning nor with the following verses. The same is true of
verses 11:45–47, which evoke Noah's intercession in favor of his son,
whereas the son was among those drowned in the flood in the preceding verses.

There also exists a particular category of interpolations deriving
from the displacement of a text within the Koran. For example, verse
24:60 commences with a rule of politeness among believers, speci-
fying that it also applies to the blind, the lame, and the sick. This precision is by all the evidence the twin of another verse, 48:17, where it
finds its real justification, since there it is a matter of authorizing these
infirm ones not to participate in war. Therefore, here in 24:60 lies a
faultily placed interpolation. The same is true of verse 28:74: ". . . the
day that Allah will call on them, He will say: 'Where are my partners,
those whom you pretended to be such?'" which has no connection
with the topics where it has been placed, except that the exact same
words are found in a preceding verse of the same surah (28:62). Here
this duplicate is followed by the response of the associated divinities,
incriminating their own idolators.

Another case of duplication, verse 35:12, seems, as Blachère has
found,[53] to take up the theme of verse 25:53 on the two seas, one sweet
and the other bitter and salty, and in its second part reiterates the theme
of verse 16:14 on the exploitation of fish in the sea. In any case, this
verse (35:12) gives the impression of an interpolation that would be
justified by an idea common to other verses, that of God's creative
power. No doubt we see here one technique in the composition of the
Koranic text, which testifies to the effect of hasty editing.

We may also speak of a mistake with regard to this verse: "We
have enjoined man to be kind to his father and mother. His mother
bore him with much pain. He is born and weaned in thirty months. /
When he grows to manhood and reaches forty years, he says: 'Lord!
Allow me to give thanks to you for the favors you have bestowed on
me as upon my father! [. . .]'" (46:15). We see here that the second part
of this verse concerns a particular person, not identified, while its

beginning tackles the general theme of the stages of human development. What person is being spoke of here? But verse 27:19 allows us to answer with near certainty: "At this, Solomon smiled and said: 'Lord! Allow me to give thanks to you for the favors you have bestowed on me as well as my father.'"[54] We see here that the author of verse 46:15 does not know the identity of the person concerned in the second part of the verse that begins with "When he grows to manhood . . ." He may even have thought that it was a general statement about human beings, which allowed him to stick it, as if it were a logical consequence, onto the first part of the verse. This mistake is manifestly of great interest for the history of the Koranic text. Could we deduce that someone other than the Prophet committed this erroneous interpolation? Quite logically, we think that must be the case since it is difficult to conceive that Muhammad would leave as authorized such a mistake. This error could only come from someone who was not sufficiently familiar with the revealed texts.

Let us signal another case held by Blachère to be a mistaken interpolation. In the very middle of the story of Moses confronting Pharaoh's magicians, there occurs a disputed verse that follows this phrase of verse 27:10: "When Messengers stand with Me, they should not be frightened of anyone." And here follows the disputed verse: "Except for those who have done wrong and then substituted good for evil, for I am forgiving and merciful" (27:11). For Blachère, it is clear that this last verse cannot refer to the "Messengers," but to sinners whose story is found elsewhere; and he argues that divine messengers could not be treated in the Koran as sinners. Yet I think that this incidental sentence is theologically correct, even if somewhat surprising in the context. The figure of Muhammad in the Koran sometimes appears as fallible: hesitant, failing to overcome those who contradict him, not to mention forgetting some verses of the Koran, or even being spoken through by Satan. Orthodox exegetes took note of all this, and they interpreted the verse in question (27:11) as referring to the messengers of Allah. That is the paradox: orthodox exegetes knew very well the truth of things—unlike modern hagiographic dogmatists.

Let us return to interpolations. There also exist glosses that serve to detail, to explain, or to add thematic developments that were not foreseen in the first redaction. For example, the long verse 7:157 introduces into the discourse addressed by God to Moses the idea of Muhammad's coming and the necessity of believing in it. This is an addition that testifies to the process of legitimation by means of the prophetic cycle.

I may also agree with Blachère in considering that the first phrase of verse 40:35—"those who dispute about the signs [âya] of Allah without any authority that has reached them"—is an interpolation aiming to explain the last phrase of the preceding verse, "Thus Allah confounds the one who is sinful and doubtful (murtâb)."[55]

Again, in the verse: "God—like the Angels and those who possess revealed knowledge—attests that / there is no divinity but him / he practices justice, [he of whom it should be said that] there is no divinity but him, the Powerful, the Wise" (3:18). We are in the presence of an interpolation of the expression in apposition "there is no divinity but him"—whose correct placement is just after "God" and not after the conjunction "that." Moreover, this interpolated part constitutes a repetition within the same verse. It is clear that the redactor of this version of the Koran has demonstrated some zeal in the glorification of God, without worrying about the grammatical or stylistic imperatives of the sentence. In any case, what is sure is that this verse has undergone the interpolation of a repetition that is wrongly placed.

In verse 2:177, there is a commentary about true pious virtue that, it is said, does not reside in the formal practice of worship but in faith and in good actions that are listed at length. When detailing these deeds, this verse switches midway through from the single mode to the plural without any justification. Why this change in number? Very probably because this change corresponds to an interpolation added by a new scribe.

We find the same phenomenon of accumulation within the same verse at 2:187, which begins by authorizing sexual relations at the breaking of the fast, then defines the limits of the day of fasting, and finally, announces an interdiction on having sexual relations inside the sacred mosque. These instructions end with this conclusion: "These are the limits (*hudûd*) set by Allah. Do not approach them to transgress them! Thus does Allah make clear his signs [*âya*] to men, hoping that perhaps they will be righteous." The last instruction about the ban on sexual relations inside the Kaaba—which was an ancient Oriental practice—shows that this verse was composed after the taking of Mecca in January 630. The first two instructions might have been revealed beforehand. The impression derived from this composition is that these three ritual prescriptions have in common either the theme of fasting or that of sexuality. No doubt the first instruction combining the two themes authorized the redactor of this verse to associate with it two other laws that each touch on one of these themes. We can see a compositional effort that was careful about the thematic order. But this order, as we see, was not logically applied, for it remains hampered by the confusion of two themes.

The verse that we are going to cite next illustrates perfectly a case of interpolation in the middle of an incidental phrase placed between a question and answer: "The Impious have not made a just estimate of Allah when they say: 'Allah did not send anything down to a mortal.' Ask them: 'Who sent down the Book brought by Moses as Light and Guide to men? / You put it into parchment rolls of which you show [little] and conceal much. You were taught what you did not know, neither you nor your ancestors.' / Say: 'It is Allah.' Then leave them to amuse themselves with their discussion" (6:91). It is remarkable that Ibn Kathîr, Ibn 'Amir, and Ubayy all give the interpolated phrases in the third person: "*They* put it into . . ." It is clear to me that this interpolation deals with the "people of the Scripture," whereas the beginning of the verse deals with the radical unbelievers, who don't believe it is possible for anything to be sent from God to humans. Blachère thinks that this interpolation must be an addition later than the emigration to Medina, and I agree with him that Ubayy's variant constitutes an attempt at harmonization with the beginning of the verse.[56]

Another example of an addition serving as an informational complement, verse 52:21 promises righteous men that in paradise they will be in the company of their children. This verse is longer than the others and breaks their rhythm. Therefore it seems that it answers a preoccupation expressed *after* the revelation of the promised paradise.

There remains one other type of possible interpolation: one that introduces a dispensation from a rule or a judgment. For example, the condemnation of poets: "The poets are followed by erring men. Do you not see how in each valley they wander and how they say what they do not do? / Except for those who have believed and who have done good works and remember Allah very much and who benefit from our help only after having been treated unjustly. Those who are unjust will know toward what destiny they are turning" (26:224–26/227–28). It is without doubt that the exception made for righteous poets that is introduced here is a belated interpolation, intended to reform a radical judgment made against poets as such. This can be more easily understood because Muhammad rallied certain poets toward the end of his apostolate, of whom the most celebrated was Hassân ibn Thâbit. Analogously, the condemnation to Gahanna of the converted of Mecca, who had refused to follow the Prophet in his emigration to Medina, finds itself nuanced in these two verses: "Except those men, women, and children who are helpless [on Earth], who have no means of escape or of finding the true path. Perhaps Allah will forgive [their faults]. Allah forgives and absolves" (4:98). The introduction of this long incidental phrase shows that we are dealing with a belated interpolation: the nuance brought in could not have been present in the text of the condemnation in verse 4:97. Similarly, when the Koran cites Abraham to the new Muslim believers as an example of someone who broke radically with his family milieu, the same verse introduces this interpolation: "Except the words of Abraham addressed to his father: 'I will indeed demand pardon for you, [but] I cannot help you against [the curse of] Allah" (60:4). It is probable that this is a response to an objection raised in the prophetic entourage about the fate of their pagan relatives. It may be also an addendum to recall the case of Abraham, who is here presented as the sole example of an attempt to save a pagan relative.

The rule pronounced in verses 24:27–28, forbidding believers to enter the houses of strangers without their authorization or when they are absent, is modified in the following verse by this derogation: "It is no fault on your part to enter uninhabited houses where there is an object belonging to you. Allah knows what you reveal and what you conceal" (24:29).

This interpolation of a dispensation sometimes ends up removing the rule's veritable raison d'être: "Seeking what the pleasurable life offers you, do not force your slaves into prostitution, in case they have made a vow of chastity! But if anyone forces them, then God, after they have been compelled, will be forgiving and merciful" (24:33). We see that the second phrase qualifies the condemnation of procurers who have been dishonest when they forced girls to prostitute themselves. All things considered, this offense has been practically absolved—after having been first condemned.

In the same way, the interdiction of taking infidels as friends (*awliyâ*) finds itself voided by the addendum "unless you have something to fear from them" (3:28). The same is true of those who have renounced their new faith. Their "reward will be the curse of Allah, the Angels and all mankind, that curse they will suffer forever, nor will their torment be lessened nor shall they be reprieved" (3:87–88). But after this severe condemnation with no possible appeal, the Koran suddenly introduces this derogation: "Except for those who afterwards repent and make amends, for Allah is forgiving and merciful" (3:89). This modification could not have been formulated at the time of the revelation of the verses of vengeance upon apostates. Only imperatives born of new power relations could have imposed such a readjustment at the last minute.

Chapter 2

THE COMPONENTS
OF THE KORAN

THE VERSES: A LATE INVENTION

The phenomenon of interpolation that we have just witnessed at work throughout these last developments has allowed us to discover the verse as the textual unit on which the Koran is based. It is time to discover its history—for it has one of its own—which is of interest in order to understand the history of the Koranic text.

The notion of a verse ought not present any historical problems. At least that is the opinion of orthodox Muslim doctrine, which has occupied itself with studying the question of the *order* of verses without wondering about their origin. Nevertheless, a division of the Koranic text into verses was only partially carried out in the most ancient Koranic manuscripts that we know of, called "Hejazian," like those in the Bibliothèque Nationale de Paris [the French National Library] cataloged as nos. 328 and 326, in which the division was introduced after they were written.[1] It is for essentially liturgical reasons that people divided the sacred text up into verses.

Our most precious source for knowing more is once again the Koran itself. It uses the term "*âya*," which is a word borrowed from Hebrew, but in a sense quite other than the one that ended up designating the textual division of the chapters of the Koran. The term "*âya*," employed 382 times in the Koran, refers essentially to a divine "sign," which might be a miraculous phenomenon, a decree, or any other manifestation of divine will and power. Among these "signs," pride of place is given to the text revealed by Allah and communicated to His prophets. Thus the Koran designates revelation by "*âya*," although often in the plural: "Allah has surely been gracious to Believers when He sent them an Apostle of their own to declare to them His *âya* (*yatlû 'alayhim âyâtihi*), to purify them . . ." (3:164). Moses was also "sent [to Pharaoh] with *âya* and a clear authority" (40:23).

As we see, this term "*âya*" is very important for understanding the nature and essence of the revealed text: it means first and foremost a divine sign, which thereby commands faith in itself and obedience to the commandments that are formulated therein.

Such, then, is the original Koranic meaning of "*âya*," which would quickly come to refer (after the death of Muhammad) to a subdivision of the chapters of the Koran. After meaning the revealed text as a divine sign, "*âya*" was reduced to a unit of textual division, a *verse*.

During the Meccan period, the criteria for the division into verses relied on style, assonance, and rhyme. An effect of style was taken by tradition as a tangible mark of the end of the verse, a *fâṣila* (plural, *fawâṣil*), or break.[2] Blachère notes in this respect that "Muslims refuse to use the word *qâfiya* (plural, *qawâfî*), or *qarîna* (plural, *qarâ'in*), to refer to Koranic rhyme, because these terms apply to poetry or the "'rhymed prose' of soothsayers."[3] The Cairo edition of the Koran contains 6,236 verses, while a tradition going back to Ibn Abbâs counts 6,616.[4] Ibn al-Arabî even recognized that the question of counting the verses of the Koran "constitutes one of the difficulties [posed by the subject] of the Koran. [For] there are so many of them that are long, while others are short, and some terminate at the end of the sentence, and others in the middle."[5] Even the opening surah, "Fātiha," has not escaped interminable debates on the number of its verses.

This uncertainty over the division into verses extends, so to speak, to the West, where the first scholarly edition of the Koran, that of Gustav Flügel (1834), cuts up certain verses of our vulgate into two or three parts, for no apparent reason. For example, verse 11:5 is subdivided into three verses (11:5–7) and a little further on, 11:7 becomes 11:9–10. Similarly, in the English translation by Marmaduke Pickthall, who followed an Indian textual tradition, verse 6:73 of the Cairo edition is divided into two parts, and 36:35–36 are combined into a single verse.

There is another difficulty linked to the arrangement of verses: the Koran underwent a major evolution in its style from the beginning of revelations until the end of Muhammad's apostolate. At the start of prophetic preaching, "The rhymed units are short and frequently marked, made up of long syllables that are strongly accentuated, offering clauses of identical rhythm."[6] Later, the tendency was to elongate the rhymed unit. The rhythm was less sustained, and remained so until the end of the preaching in Mecca, where the rhythmic unit becomes rare while being stretched across multiple sentences.[7] Because of this, the verse assumed increasingly large proportions, going from a single word, as in verse 89:1, to the extreme of covering a whole page in 2:282.

If the division into verses—starting with its modes and its history—is destined to remain always a problem, neither do we know the process that presided over the establishment of their order. Here, official doctrine is clear: "The order of verses was fixed by [Muhammad] and on his command, and there is no divergence on this point among Muslims," declared Suyûtî, according to uncontested authorities.[8] Caliph Uthmân is said to have reported that "as soon something from the Koran comes down to Muhammad, he calls a scribe and tells him to 'put these verses in the *surah* that speaks of such-and-such.'"[9] One other tradition specifies that Muhammad put the verses into order according to the express instructions of Gabriel.[10] Sometimes, this archangel of revelation gives this order directly to the collectors of the Koran: "Put this verse in that place,"[11] thereby contradicting the thesis that makes Muhammad the one who has chosen the order of verses. Moreover, Suyûṭî explains that the companions were listening to the Prophet recite certain surahs during prayers, and concluded that it would be quite normal for them to keep the same order for the verses during the elaboration of the Koran compendiums.[12] Nevertheless, a little later, Suyûṭî reports that it is Umar who has decided on the placing of the two last verses of the surah *barâ'a* (9:128–29). Umar even goes so far as to say that if these two verses had been three in number, then he would have made them into a separate surah.[13] In fact, the order of the verses was not definitively fixed until quite late, no doubt in the Umeyyad era.

THE SURAHS

The surah (*sûra*) is a term universally accepted, since the time of most ancient writings on the history of the Koran, to designate the major divisions of the Koranic text, that is to say, its chapters. However, this term is used in the Koran with a meaning that scarcely covers the idea of a textual division, but rather only a text. Let us take two examples: "Those who believe say: If only a *surah* were revealed! But when a forthright *surah* (*muhkama*) is revealed and the order to make war is mentioned in it . . ." (47:20). "The Hypocrites are afraid lest a *surah* should be revealed to them proclaiming what is in their hearts" (9:64), and so on.

    With only one exception, the nine occurrences of the word "*sûra*" in the Koran are associated with the term for "descending" (of a revelation, i.e., *'unzila*) and involve the idea of written text. This definition perfectly conforms to its Syriac origin, "*sûrtâ*," which is translated as

"Scripture, reading of Scripture."[14] Thus, in Koranic usage, "*sûra*" designates an "*âya*," but only in its textual aspect. In fact both refer to a unit of revelation: a text communicated in the course of a revelation. For in effect, the original division of the Koranic text is constituted by a series of texts revealed during oracular experiences, in the course of which God communicates (during each one) a revelation on a precise theme and for a precise purpose. We could say that therein lies the only textual unity that is natural and original to the Koran as revelation. It was only later that people contemplated aggregating these revealed texts—either in order to complete prior revelations or for editorial reasons—by gathering them into chapters.

Thus, each chapter generally encompasses a multitude of revelations with different themes. But each of these revelations was originally called a "*sûra*," that is to say, a unit of revelation received in the course of one of the oracular experiences from which the Koranic texts sprang. It was only at a much later date that "*sûra*" began to designate a chapter. Let us take the example of chapter 24, "*al-Nûr*" ("The Light"). Its preamble gives this information: "[Here is] a *sûra* which We have revealed and sanctioned, wherein We have revealed explicit signs [*âya*], so that you may take heed" (24:1). As we see, the placement here of the word "*sûra*" gives the current reader the illusion that it refers to the whole chapter concerned, with its subdivision into *âyât*, or verses. But this is only an illusion. This introduction tells us that this *sûra* is "sanctioned (*faraznâha*)," an explicit allusion to the penal arrangements laid out in the nine verses that immediately follow it. Consequently, it appears that the *sûra* refers only to these nine verses. And the "explicit *âya* (*bayyinât*)" that this *sûra* is supposed to contain does not refer to the verses in general, but precisely to the decrees announced in this introduction, which is one of the original meanings of *âya*. Thus, here we see clearly the meaning given to *sûra*: a unit of oracular revelation and not a chapter, that is, an editorial unit.

After the series of decrees announced in the preamble to surah 24 comes a thematic development on the affair in which Aïsha, the Prophet's wife, was accused of adultery (verses 11–26). But the decrees 2 to 10, announced in the preamble, concern precisely the punishments awaiting false accusers of adultery. We see here a thematic addition with respect to the historical context for the decrees. There follow some injunctions about social conduct. And then, a first preamble explains a parable on the divine light, followed by a hymn to Allah. Still another preamble launches a polemic against the opponents of Medina. Finally, once again come instructions on good conduct. It is clear that the term "*sûra*" in the first introductory verse concerns, at least originally, not the surah in its current composition—that is, an ensemble of revelations gathered into a specific chapter—but precisely one revelation, this one here, concerning the decrees cited in verses 2–10.

Here in fact we are touching on some elements that will enlighten us about the emergence of chapters as collections of these units of revelations.

The composition of the surah "*al-Nûr*" that we have just detailed shows that the actual surah as we have it is an aggregate of revelations, whether or not they are introduced in the form of an announcement. The question that might be posed now is whether there are preambles designed to cover the *whole* of the actual surah. This question amounts to asking if certain of the introductory formulas were introduced *after* the formation of the series of revelations gathered into a surah.

THE PREAMBLES

First let us look more closely at these preambles that serve to introduce certain chapters of the Koran. Immediately we see that some of these introductions begin with a series of letters of the alphabet that we will study later.

A good number of these introductory formulas are announcements about the nature of the revelation: a text called "*Qur'ân*" (Preaching/ Recitation) is drawn from a "*kitâb*" (celestial original). "A.L.M. This Scripture (*dhâlika al-kitâb*) is not to be doubted. It is a guide for the

Righteous" (2:1–2). "A.L.M.S. [This is] a Book (*kitâb*) that has been revealed to you . . ." (7:1–2). "A.L.R. These are revelations/verses (*âya*) of the wise Book (*kitâb*)" (10:1; 31:1–2 also carries "A.L.M."). "A.L.R. A Book (*kitâb*) whose verses (*âya*) are perfected and then expounded by He who is wise and all-knowing" (11:1). "A.L.R. These are the *âya* of the glorious *kitâb*, which We have revealed in a recitation (*qur'ân*) in Arabic, so that you may understand it" (12:1–2). "Ḥ.M. [This is] a *kitâb* revealed by the Compassionate and Merciful. A *kitâb* whose *âya* are expounded. It is an Arabic *Qur'ân* for people of knowledge" (41:1–3). "Ṭ.S.M. These are the *âya* of the glorious *kitâb*" (26:1–2 and 28:1–2). "T.S. These are the *âya* of the *Qur'ân* and a glorious *kitâb*" (27:1). "H. M. By the glorious *kitâb*! We have revealed a *Qur'ân* in the Arabic language so that you may understand its meaning. And it is found in the Mother of Scripture in our keeping. [Allah] is sublime and full of wisdom" (43:1–4). "A.L.M.R. These are the *âya* of the *kitâb*. What has been revealed to you by your Lord is the Truth, yet most people do not believe" (13:1). "A.L.R. [This is] a *kitâb* that We have revealed to you so that, by their Lord's will, people will escape from Darkness into Light, and come to the path of the Mighty One worthy of Praise" (14:1). These preambles, explaining the heavenly provenance of the recitation/*qur'ân*, function as certificates of authenticity of the revelations in general, and of the ones they introduce in particular.

Another type of preamble announces the theme tackled immediately thereafter. We have seen an illustration of this in surah 24 (*al-Nûr*) that we have just examined. Other preambles have the same characteristic: "[This is a] reminder of your Lord's goodness to his servant Zachariah" (19:2). And in fact surah 19 (called *Maryam*) deals with the story of the annunciations made to Zachariah and to Mary of the coming of Jesus. This portion (in forty verses) is followed by another twenty-two verses devoted to Abraham, Moses, Ishmael, and Idris. The rest of this chapter is formed of thirty-four verses that respond to arguments from nonbelievers. Here again, the preamble concerns only the first revelation of the surah. It is clear that the original *sûra* has been augmented a posteriori by several other *sûras* (in the first meaning of this term). In this case, we can no longer know if these additions were made in Muhammad's lifetime or afterward.

And as in surah 24, this nineteenth surah called "*Maryam*" is interrupted midway through by a fresh preamble. In effect, the last group of thirty-four verses is introduced by this preamble: "We descend [or, according to a variant, "And the *kitâb* descended"] only at the bidding of your Lord. To Him belongs all that is before Us, what is behind Us, and what is between the two. Your Lord is not forgetful. He is Lord of the Heavens and the Earth and all that is between them. Therefore worship Him and be constant in adoring Him! Do you know any other worthy of His name?" (19:64–65).

This is incontestably a typical preamble, comparable to those placed at the beginning of certain chapters. This is all the more true because this introductory formula of revelation contains the two themes specific to preambles: 1) the announcement of a *qur'ân* deriving from a celestial *kitâb*, which is 2) followed by the mention of the omnipotence of God, and especially of His power to create the world and humankind, or the mention of His quality of possessing the world or of providing the subsistence of beings living on Earth, or else His capacity for destruction, and so on.

These two themes are recurrent in most of the preambles, as in: "T.H. We have not revealed the Qur'ân to distress you [but] only [as] a reminder to the one who fears Allah [and as] a revelation coming from Him who created the earth and the lofty heavens" (20:1–4). "A.L.M. [This] Scripture is revealed—beyond all doubt—by the Lord of the Universe. Do they say: 'He has invented it'? Not at all! It is the Truth emanating from your Lord so that you may forewarn a nation whom none has warned before you, that they may be rightly guided. Allah it is who created the heavens and the earth . . ." (32:1–4). "H.M. By the glorious *kitâb*! We revealed it on a blessed night. We are ever warning, and on this night, every decree is made plain . . . God of the Heavens, of the earth and all that is between, if only you knew this" (44:1–4, 7). "H.M. '.S.Q. Thus He has inspired [you] and those who came before you. To God the Mighty and Wise belong what is on heaven and on earth" (42:1–4). Sometimes, the creative power of Allah is expressed without mention of "heaven and earth": "Ḥ.M. This *kitâb* is revealed by God the Mighty and Omniscient" (39:1). "This *kitâb* is revealed by God the Mighty, the Wise" (45:1–2, 46:1–2).

Regarding preambles, let us note that the case of surah 3 (*The Family of Imrân*) begins with this formula: "A.L.M. Allah—there is no God but Him—who is Living and Eternal. He has revealed to you the *kitâb* with the Truth ..." (3:1–2). Here the formula is inverted, since it begins with an invocation of divine attributes. And we may observe that this formula—"Allah—there is no God but him—who is Living and Eternal"—is a reproduction of the introduction to verse 2:255, called the Verse of the Throne, one of the verses most revered by Muslims. Is this a clue that might show that certain preambles were composed on the model provided by previous revelations?

THE MYSTERIOUS LETTERS

These preambles are not the only tangible elements that mark the start of *sûras*. Other and even more significant elements exist. These are the famous and mysterious letters that we have just read above at the beginning of the preambles. Tradition designates these letters as *fawâtîḥ* or *awâ'il al-suwar* (*incipit* of surahs), or *al aḥruf al-muqattaʿa* (isolated letters). Many hypotheses have been put forth, both by Muslim Tradition and in the West, in order to explain these letters. Some have recognized in them precedents from numerology. Others see them as abbreviations of divine names, or of historical and geographical names, or even of the titles of surahs.

But what is important for our argument is that studying the recurrence of different groups of letters, especially "A.L.M.," "A.L.R.," "Ṭ.S.M.," and "Ḥ.M.," shows an evident link with the current order of the surahs, on the one hand, and with the presence of preambles at the start of certain surahs, on the other. It is impossible to deny in these conditions the role played by these mysterious letters in the process of the elaboration of surahs as subdivisions of the Koran. These letters, for us as for those who elaborated the definitive text of the Koran, amount to criteria for the classification of surahs.

Whatever the reasons that governed the choice of these letters, they were not designated by any such appellation in the Koranic text, like the concepts of *âya* and *sûra*, as elements of the Koranic text. Moreover, it does not seem to me that the Koran alludes to them in the preambles, contrary to the opinion of A. T. Welch,[15] who wrote an excellent summary of the question in *The Encyclopedia of Islam*. Welch stands alongside Loth, Nöldeke, Schwally, Bell, and Alan Jones in considering that the mysterious letters are an integral part of the revelation.

In fact, these letters, as we have seen, are linked to a process of classification of verses, as even Welch himself well demonstrates. But, in my opinion, originally these letters were *not* designed to identify the surahs.

Welch has shown that all the mysterious letters were selected according to a criterion relating to the writing of the Arabic alphabet in the time of Muhammad. In effect, the Arabic alphabet did not possess the diacritical signs that allow a distinction between certain consonants that have the same shape. Thus, the letters *b*, *t*, *th*, and *n* were written all in the same manner and nothing distinguished one from another until, after several centuries, a reform introduced signs over these letters that finally permitted them to be differentiated. What is remarkable about the mysterious letters is that they include only univocal notations, and in the case of letters whose notation necessitates diacritical signs, a single letter was chosen. Thus, in the example that I have cited, the *y* was used to the exclusion of other letters. This choice is of course arbitrary. But it is clear that a choice cannot be made unless reading is associated with memory, for as we must remember, nothing distinguished its notation from other similar letters.

Thus we have proof that the mysterious letters were chosen from the perspective of the Koranic texts being put into writing. In my opinion, this is sufficient proof to assert that these letters have a direct link to the process of the formation of surahs.

A new track of clues, which I would like to mention here briefly, might shed some light on the relation between the mysterious letters and the constitution of surahs. It relates to the codicological practice contemporary with Muhammad, by which the letters of the alphabet were in effect used to mark the gatherings that comprised the codices. Georges Ifrah, who has worked on the history of numbers, remarks that "in serto [or Jacobite, one of three forms of Syriac writing], as in Nestorian, the letters have served, and sometimes still serve in our day, as signs of numeration, which is confirmed by the fact that, in all the Syriac manuscripts (at least those that are later than the 9th century), the gatherings that constitute the codex are all regularly numbered in such a way as to avoid any error—of omission or introversion—in making up the 'book'. The numerical value of the Syriac letters is exactly the same as among the Jews: the first nine ones are associated with single digits, the nine succeeding ones with tens, and the four last with four first hundreds."[16]

And in effect the mysterious letters must have seen the light of day *after* the redaction of the compendiums of revealed texts. These compendiums had to conform to the practice proper to the organization of codices of the time, to wit, the insertion at the head of the collection of an introduction containing a brief announcement of its content. These are the preambles of surahs.

It is important to note in this respect that the principal personage entrusted with the collection of the Koran in the time of the first caliphs was Zayd ibn Thâbit, one of the last secretaries of Muhammad. It is reported that he "knew how to write Syriac."[17] This indication is obviously of great importance and it might plead in favor of the Syriac codicological avenue as the model of the elaboration of Koranic compendiums in the time of the Prophet, and even afterward.

This practice of using preambles is even attested in the Essene writings from the Dead Sea that date from six to seven centuries before Muhammad. Thus, the *Book of Blessings* has as its preamble: "Words of benediction for the intelligent man, in order to bless those who fear God and do his will . . ."[18] We see that this formula is strangely similar to those Koranic preambles examined above. In the same way, the type of Koranic exordium that begins with "This is a writing . . ." is found in the prologue to the *Book of Jubilees*: "This is the story of the legal and certified division of time . . ."[19] Finally, let me mention the exordium to a text from Qumrân: "Word of blessing from Enoch. Thus he blesses the elect and the righteous who will see on the day of anguish the extermination of all enemies and the salvation of the righteous."[20] There is a strange affinity here between this text from the start of the Christian era and the Koran. The genre of the Koranic preamble manifestly belongs to an old Oriental literary tradition.

The second codicological practice is the signature of the notebooks [cahiers], which consists of assigning them numerical letters. Generally these letters appear in the "upper external angle, which is where a signature was most frequently placed in ancient manuscripts until the middle of the 11th century."[21] The first Koranic sheets certainly did receive such signatures, that is to say, a numeration by means of letters. During the copying of these first notebooks, the scribes must have had the habit of reproducing these letters that appeared at the head of the manuscript, either out of a concern to identify the surah, or in the belief that they were part of the revealed text. Those surahs bearing the same combination of letters might originally have been part of the same notebook signed with the same letters. Thus, the constitution of surahs in their current aspect would be partly the result of fragmentation in copying the first long compendiums into more reduced notebooks.

Moreover, this fragmentation might be comprehended from the fact that the new Muslim community did not stop growing and enlarging, and therefore required more access to the sacred texts, which were serving as aids for oral learning. These new needs must have been more easily satisfied by breaking up the first long compendiums into more lightweight ones, more suitable for quicker and wider distribution. This shift could only have taken place thanks to a multiplication in the number of reciters (*qurrâ'*) whose need for sheets was growing. It was only in a third stage that there was the opposite tendency to gather into a single compilation these fragmented surahs. This last phase corresponded to the constitution of the book that today we know under the name of the Koran, *al-Qur'ân*, and whose presumed "collection," according to Tradition, did not take place until well after the death of the Prophet.

Of course, during this last phase, the Prophet was no longer there to authorize the major structural editing that affected the texts as they were being written during his lifetime. All that could be done touched on the placement of those *suras*—in the first Koranic sense of the term—that had not been classified in the first compilations (phases 1 and 2) and hence were not identified by the introductory formula and/or by the signature-letters. These wandering surahs were either inserted into the compilations of phase 2 (that of the fragmentary collections), or else they were constituted as independent surahs, either grouped or standing alone. Undoubtedly it was in the course of this phase 3 of the constitution of our actual vulgate that the mysterious letters lost their primary importance, since from now on a large number of "unsigned" texts are found.

For if there exist only 29 surahs provided with such groups of letters out of a total of 114, this is due, as we have seen, largely to the chance circumstances of the duplication of the first compilations and to the uncertain awareness that the copyists of this second phase possessed the status of these letters. One proof is that surah 39 is placed in a group having the same letters (Ḥ.M.) and the same preamble as it does—except that it is deprived of these letters. So why have the latter disappeared from the vulgate, whereas other recensions like those of Ubayy have kept them?

Moreover, Welch has shown that "most of the groups of letters, when you spell them, introduce the rhyme of the surahs concerned."[22] In any case, this correspondence illustrates the original link that existed between the preambles and the first verses (only) of the actual surahs.

THE DIVISION OF SURAHS

The history of the constitution of the actual surahs is evidently complex, since it proceeded by means of divisions of the initial compilations and later regroupings. Under these conditions we should not be at all surprised to observe some preambles actually inside surahs. This is the case of surah 19, where we have noted the existence of a preamble in its middle, at verses 19:64–65, which is the trace of the integration of one collection into another.

Let us take the case of manifest hesitation in integrating surah 9—called "*al-tawba*" or "*barâ'a*"—into its precursor, surah 8, called "*al-'anfâl*." The most tangible sign of this hesitation is the absence of the *basmala* at the head of surah 9, the only one so deprived in the entire Koran. An explanation of this hesitation is attributed to Caliph Uthmân: "[The surah] *al-'anfâl* was among the first to be revealed in Medina, and *al-barâ'a* was among the last of the surahs revealed. Due to the fact that the two surahs are similar in theme, I believed that surah 9 belonged to 8. And the Prophet died without confirming this to us. For this reason I did not separate the two surahs by the formula of the *basmala*."[23]

Blachère observes that these two surahs were first joined to each other during the classification of surahs according to their decreasing length. Thus, he explains, we have the following sequence: surah 7 takes up thirty-four pages (of the Cairo edition); surah 8 has thirteen pages; surah 9 has twenty-six pages; surah 10 has eighteen pages. He deduces from this that surahs 8 and 9 were welded together during this putting into order.[24]

Two other cases of division of one group of revelations into two are reported by Tradition and concern brief surahs arranged at the end of the vulgate. Ubayy's collection had presented surahs 105 (*al-Fîl*) and 106 (*Quraysh*) as a single surah.[25] It is related that in the course of a prayer, Caliph Umar recited the two surahs without separating them by the formula of the *basmala* "in the name of Allah, the Merciful Benefactor."[26]

According to al-Râzî (850–923 CE), surahs 93 ("*al-Dhuḥâ*") and 94 ("*'Alam nashraḥ*") had been originally a single one.[27]

We note also that surah 103 ("The Declining Day") was originally only a fragment that could not be integrated into other surahs. In addition, its verse 3 is manifestly a later addition, since it constitutes a development that differs in length very significantly from the two first verses.

Other cases of the integration of some surahs into others may be remarked, like the development that commences in verse 6:92: "And this is a blessed Scripture that we have revealed, confirming what came before it . . ." Like the other preambles, this theme about scripture is followed by an exposition of divine omnipotence. Similarly, one may observe in certain short surahs a very clear aggregation of numerous original surahs, as in surah 80 ("*'Abasa*"), which makes up only a page but is composed of no fewer than four independent subject developments: the first on the incident when the Prophet despised a blind person, the second on Koranic revelation, the third on the arrogance of humanity, and the last on an apocalyptic description of the Day of Last Judgment. These four developments might well have consituted independent surahs, but no doubt accidents in the history of the transmission of collections ultimately imposed this composition—which is, as we have seen, far from an isolated case.

Similarly, one may observe in verses 75 onward of surah 56 ("*al-wâqi'a*," "The Event") a whole development that begins with a vigorous oath typical of the start of certain Meccan surahs and continues with a genre specific to preambles, the affirmation of the authenticity of scripture (*kitâb*). It is clear here that the first Koranic compilations were not interested in marking a separation between the revealed parts. This explains the numerous cases of preambles integrated without separation in the midst of actual surahs.

Above we saw the inverse case of surah 9 called "Repentance" ("*al-tawba*"), the only one in the whole vulgate without the propitiatory formula of the *basmala*. This might be a matter of an accidental separation due to mistakes in the editing of the copies, unless the omission of the *basmala* was also not accidental, for errors by copyists were by no means rare.

We may illustrate the latter phenomenon on page 295 of the Kufic manuscript called Samarkand that dates from the second century of the Hijra. Within surah 6 ("*al-anʿâm*," "Herd"), a development typical of preambles starts at verse 92 in these terms: "This is a blessed Scripture that we have revealed . . ." What is remarkable in this manuscript is that the scribe has proceeded as if it were a matter of the start of a surah. On the one hand, he began this verse at the start of the line, leaving an empty space in the preceding line, while nothing justifies such an arrangement, not even any canonic division at this placement. On the other hand, the coordinating conjunction "*wa*" was omitted, reinforcing the impression of the start of a surah. We see here clearly the scribe's hesitation to remodel the division of surahs by following his own instinct. The omission of the *basmala* in surah 9 might originally have been only a mistake deriving from an error by the copyist, comparable to the one we just saw in the manuscript of Samarkand.

THE *BASMALA* AND *AL-RAHMÂN*

The surahs contained in the actual book of the Koran are all preceded, except for surah 9 ("Repentance"), by the liturgical formula, *bismi allâhi al-rahmâni al-rahîmi*, which might be translated as "In the name of Allah, the Merciful Benefactor" (Blachère), or as "In the name of God lenient and merciful" (Paret). It is evident, after what I have just said on the subject of the gradual formation of surahs, that this formula could not have been considered as being part of the surahs until after their composition.

This might be proved by other considerations. First of all, as Welch demonstrated, the first Koranic revelations referred to God as *rabb* (Lord). It was only in the second period that the names "Allah" and "*al-Rahmân*" appeared (with even a preference for the latter, for example, in surah 19, where "*al-Rahmân*" is cited sixteen times).

Verse 17:110 authorizes Muslims to use the two names of God: "Say: call on *Allah* or call on *al-Rahmân*! By whatever name you call on Him, His are the most gracious names." This verse might be explained by the debate (related in Tradition) on the subject of the rejection by certain Qurayshite companions of the use of the name *al-Rahmân*, who preferred the name *Allah*. No doubt it was after these incidents that *al-Rahmân* became less and less used as a name for God in the revealed texts.[28]

Let us note here that the name *"Rahmân"* is the name of a south Arabian divinity. It was assimilated in the west Semitic domain to *Hadad*, the god of thunder. Musaylima, who pretended to prophesize in the time of Muhammad, was directly inspired by this same god *al-Rahmân*. The debate over the name of God might have had a direct or indirect relation with the dissidence of Musaylima, who was executed by the prestigious military leader Khâlid ibn al-Walîd during a military expedition ordered by the first caliph of Islam, Abû Bakr, after the death of the Prophet. In addition, we find the story of Musaylima curiously mentioned in the context of the collecting of the Koran, since certain accounts explain that the decision to undertake it was taken as a result of the death of a great number of readers of the Koran in the course of the battle waged against this "false" prophet. This battle might perhaps have been the culmination of a disagreement that went back to the debate over the god *al-Rahmân* and that would have needed sanction from the new powers to refine an official text that might ratify this victory and prevent the revelations of Musaylima being considered as canonical. This danger was all the more real because Muhammad had adopted an attitude, as we have seen, of reconciliation with *al-Rahmân*.

And so there might have been a certain relation between the elimination of Musaylima and the commencement of the formation of a Koranic canon. Al-Kindî, a Christian Arabic author of the eighth and ninth centuries of the Common Era, replies to a Muslim opponent on the subject of the inimitability of the Koran that he had held in his hands a compilation of the revelations of Musaylima: "You cannot disregard that men such as Musaylima al-Ḥanafî, al-Aswad al-ʿAnasî, Tulayhâ al-Asadî, and so many others, produced works similar to that of your master. I attest, for my part, that I have read a collection by Musaylima that, had it appeared, might have brought several of your friends to renounce Islam. But these men had no support, as was the case for your master."[29]

Quite evidently, we do not know if the *basmala* was present in Musaylima's compilation, but Muslim Tradition was reluctant to count the *basmala* as a verse, even if the current vulgate considers it such. According to Tradition, some compilations of the Koran assimilated this formula into a verse, thus increasing the total number of Koranic verses by 114. In his *Kitâb al-kashf*, al-Qaysî, who relayed this fact, rejected this practice as not conforming to the consensus among the companions of the Prophet or to the view of their immediate successors.[30] In fact, two important legal schools defended opposing doctrines: the legal advisers of Medina, Basra, and Syria refused to grant the *basmala* a verse status, reducing it to a simple editorial technique serving in the Koranic codices to separate the surahs, or at most as a formula of benediction. By contrast, the Shafi'ite legal advisers of Mecca and Kûfa considered the *basmala* as a verse in and of itself, and they recited it aloud.[31]

But a very interesting indication exists about the place of the *basmala* in the origins of Islam. In effect, Tradition concerning the reading of the Koran informs us that Muhammad did not recite the *basmala* when he read the surahs one after another.[32] For his part, Ḥamza, who was one of the seven canonical readers, is said not to have pronounced the *basmala* formula between surahs. Al-Qaysî, who reported this, gives this explanation for it: "The *basmala* was not for him—nor in the opinion of the jurists—considered a verse, he omitted it during the passage from one surah to the other, in order that one would not suppose that it constituted a verse situated at the start of the surah. For him, the Koran was, in its totality, taken as a single surah. . . . Its presence in the collected Koran was only a means to indicate that one surah was terminated and that another was beginning."[33]

These indications, one sees, are very instructive about the liturgical function of the *basmalas* when they were first used. It was only relatively late, during the "collection" phase of the Koranic text, that a *basmala* ended up being attached to each of the surahs. This evolution is thus similar to the fate of the mysterious letters that figured at the head of the first collections, which, reproduced and recombined during the splitting up of these first collections, had thereby lost their initial function. In both cases, there is a tendency to fix and integrate into the revealed text some elements that at the start were not part of it and had quite different uses.

THE TITLES OF SURAHS

We would say just the same thing about the titles of surahs, which were perfectly integrated into the copies of the Koran from the beginnings of Islam down to the present day. Nevertheless, these titles do not figure in the first known Koranic manuscripts. Their absence results from the very history of the constitution of the revelations in surahs, a hazardous history that, as we have seen, resulted only very late in the current concept of the surah. Moreover, the signature-letters were meant to fulfill the function of title until a very late date. But we have seen that this system pertained only to the first phase of the collection of revelations into anthologies. The fractioning of the latter meant that several surahs bore the same letters, without anyone trying to differentiate them. Nevertheless, it seems that there were some attempts in this direction, as in the passage from A.L.M. to A.L.M.S̲., or to A.L.M.R. But this phenomenon remained rare. Letters could no longer fulfill the function of title—hence the recourse to other designations, which were elaborated in a very improvised way, since numerous surahs had several denominations from the start, as illustrated by Suyûtî in his chapter on the "Names of Surahs."[34] A title is often a key word that marks the surah, either because it is found there exclusively, or because it evokes a particular theme. Sometimes one even utilizes the mysterious letters of the surah to designate it, which is normally only a return to the sources.

Tradition, according to Suyûṭî, tried to make the titles of surahs date back to the Prophet, who is said to have fixed them.[35] Yet the same Suyûṭî reports in the following paragraph that a tradition has Anas ibn Mâlik, celebrated companion of the Prophet, say: "Never say 'Surah of the Cow', nor 'Surah the Family of Imrân', nor 'Surah of the Women' etc., but say: 'the surah where the Cow is mentioned', or 'the surah where the Imrân family is described,' etc." And Suyûṭî hastens to remark that this tradition is not certain.[36] This testimony confirms that the adoption of the actual titles of surahs did not prevail until after many hesitations, and that these titles were not integrated into the corpus of revelation until quite late—later, even, than the mysterious letters.

Recent codicological research has demonstrated an evolution in the formula of presentation of the titles of surahs within the mass of fragments of manuscripts from Sanaa, Yemen, discovered recently (1972). Bothmer, who has studied these manuscripts, observes that the first scribes (at the end of the first century of the Hijra) utilized this formula at the end of the surah: "End of *sûra* X," after the model of the first Christian manuscripts of the Bible.[37] Then the formula became "End of *sûra* X and start of *sûra* Y (*khâtimatu sûrat X wa fâtihatu sûrat Y*)." Later, the formula was reduced to its initial part— "Start of *sûra* X"—and then it became stable with simply "*sûra* X." Thus, the indicative formula of surahs changed places, migrating from the end of the surah to its beginning. Of course, all this evolution was merely the final phase of a previous evolution that saw the gradual formation of the titles of surahs.

Chapter 3

WRITINGS OF
THE KORAN

This fixing of the redactional elements of the Koran was performed gradually and in several stages. Still, the collection of
the Koran remains a complex phenomenon surrounded in deep obscu-
rity. This phenomenon is due not only to the extreme indigence of our
paleographic documentation, but also to the very nature of the revelation and its relation to the text.

We have seen how the preambles and letter-signs that accompany
them were imposed on the Koranic text on account of external needs,
purely editorial and scriptural, that conformed to the practices of the
time.

The same is true of the very project to collect the Koran, which
was accepted tacitly as an imperative, inscribed within the logic of a
scriptural revelation, whereas the project of "a book" came about only
a posteriori, once the revelation was complete.

Even the very idea of gathering the scattered texts of the revelation into a collection, according to stories reported by tradition, had been received with amazement: "How, exclaimed Caliph Abû Bakr, would I dare to do something that the Prophet did not do?"[1] This was how he responded to Umar, who had suggested this project, as we have just seen, after the death of a great number of reciters of the Koran during the battle of Yamâma, in which the Muslims fought Musaylima, the false prophet. Abû Bakr, who ended up accepting this project, designated Zayd ibn Thâbit, one of the Prophet's secretaries, to carry out this audacious enterprise. But the latter was in turn scandalized and is said to have made the same response as Abû Bakr had given to Umar. But Zayd, too, ended up accepting the task.

How can we explain this astonishment of the first Muslims at the idea of gathering the revealed texts into a single volume? For this *is* an "astonishing" astonishment, if we consider that it is expressed by the greatest companion of the Prophet and a witness to the first ordering of the divine revelations. We—for whom it is so evident today that "the" Koran can be read at a single sitting, that it can be leafed through with a simple gesture—cannot even imagine that such a sacred text could once have been presented scattered into dozens of sheets without any organic link and without any prospect of unity. It is clear that this astonishment attests to the fact that among the first Muslims, the companions of the Prophet, a sort of revolution was taking place in the perception of the revealed texts, held until then as units autonomous in their meanings, now to propose to turn them suddenly into a new and unsuspected-of entity. Revelation had been plural, and now it was being proposed to construct from its elements something unprecedented: "a" Koran.

Our Koran in effect restores to us the scattered and plural structure of revelation, materialized in numerous written supports. In addressing Muhammad on the subject of revelation, Allah had been precise that the revelation contained seven parts: "We have given you the seven *mathânî* [oft-repeated verses?] and the Glorious *Qur'ân*" (15:87). It is difficult to determine the nature of these revealed units called *mathânî*, but what is certain is that they introduce a plural structure of revealed themes. When the Koran speaks of revelations prior to the Koran, each one is also referred to in the plural. In verse 6:91, the Jews are reproached for hiding certain scrolls of parchment (*qarâtîs*) among the ensemble of scrolls in which was kept the scripture (*kitâb*) revealed to Moses. There is also a reference to *suhuf* (sheets) with regard to the Apocrypha attributed to Abraham and Moses: *suhuf ibrâhîma wa mûsâ* (53:36; 87:19). The multiplicity of supports, here the *suhuf*, is reflected, so to speak, in the multiplicity of supports for the original heavenly one, also designated by *suhuf*. These are characterized as "venerated, exalted and purified in the hands of noble and innocent Scribes" (80:13–16). These same "purified *suhuf*" are supposed to contain "infallible scriptures (*kutub qayyima*)" (98:3).

We see that revelation is not presented as a unitary composition but always in the form of compilations, each containing multiple revelations, in conformity with their original celestial form. In these conditions, we can understand that an enterprise to collect the revealed texts into an ensemble obeying a certain nonrevealed order might have shocked some people and appeared as a veritable distortion of revelation—in short, a *bid'a*, an intervention foreign to divine will.

It is remarkable in this respect that the stories that have come down to us on the history of the collecting of the Koran give justifications for it that are purely accidental. When Umar suggested such an enterprise to Caliph Abû Bakr, it was after the battle against Musaylima. Thus this event is not continuous with the history of the text revealed in the time of the Prophet. According to this logic, if people who were the holders of the Koranic text had not died a violent death, there would not have been a project of collection. For, strictly speaking, it was not necessary to resort to a written collection in order to assure the conservation of revealed texts: it sufficed to constitute a corps of reciters of the Koran to palliate the risk of such a breakdown of transmission, accidental or not. And whatever the case, given the deficient character of Arabic writing at this time, a recourse to writing did not seem the most adequate and most effective solution, since, in any case, one would have need of a "reader" of this writing.

It is clear this logic that had presided over the initiative to collect all the revealed texts was not taking advantage of continuity with any past that it was seeking to culminate, quite simply because this past did not imply such a culmination. And the idea of a general and entire collection of all the revelations had no place in the representation that was made during Muhammad's lifetime of the textual composition of the revelation. It was presented in the form of a certain number of compilations that contained a greater or lesser number of revelations. This satisfied everybody and there was no theological or historical reason whatever to proceed with such a written collection.

The project of such a book, while harmonizing ever so slightly revelation in the plural, was certainly not among the scriptural habits of the epoch. One could not reproach Muhammad for not having been able to foresee such a book and not having made the necessary arrangements in order to leave us a complete copy, which might have avoided his successors having to take the initiative of proceeding to a collection, a task as heavy as it was risky. In these circumstances, do we have to believe (as does Blachère) in "this particularity of the Arab soul that, absorbed in what is immediate, never anticipates the future. Nobody thought of constituting the Koranic corpus because nobody felt the necessity of doing so during Muhammad's lifetime"?[2] Or do we have to explain this deficiency by an imminent eschatological perspective that would have rendered such an enterprise useless, as Casanova has suggested?[3] But this would be making the error of anachronism. The idea of "a book" did not germinate until quite late, and for reasons that no longer had any link whatsoever with the prophetic era.

Blachère is perfectly right to remark that Abû Bakr's collection could not have served much purpose, since once the Koranic text was consigned to "sheets," nobody felt the need to consult it. Tradition tells us in effect that it was deposited with the caliph, and that at his death it passed to his successor, Umar, and then to his daughter Hafsa, widow of the Prophet.[4] Thus the text does not seem to have had any great utility to the new Muslim community then being born, and in any case it was not of much help in remedying the problems of transmission that were believed to be detected after the death of certain reciters of the Koran.

This situation did not last long, since (still according to Tradition) the collection of the Koran was once again put on the agenda in the time of the third caliph, Uthmân. The reason that motivated this resurgence of interest in shaping the Koran was this time of a technical nature. According to the predominant version of the facts, in the course of a military expedition in Armenia and Azerbaijan, there was an argument between Iraqi and Syrian soldiers over the way to recite the Koran, which brought their military leader to ask Caliph Uthmân to unify the reading of the sacred text. So he ordered to be delivered to him the copy established by Abû Bakr that had remained in the hands of Hafsa, and he had it submitted to a commission for the purpose of making a certain number of copies to distribute to the different capitals of the Muslim Empire: Kûfa, Basra, Damascus, and Mecca. Uthmân also ordered the destruction of all the other existing copies, with the exception of that of Hafsa, whose copy was given back to her.

This was because it was perceived that, in parallel with Hafsa's copy, a rather large number of other private collections had meanwhile been made: those belonging to the future caliph Umar, Sâlim ibn Ma'qil, who had outlived Muhammad by only a year; to Abdallah ibn Abbâs, cousin of the Prophet; Oqba ibn 'Âmir, another companion of the Prophet, whose copy was still extant in the fourth century (H); Miqdâd ibn 'Amr, who died in the year 33 (H) with his recension known especially in Syria; Abû Mûsa al-Ash'ari, who died in 52 with his recension known in Bassora; Caliph Ali, cousin of the Prophet, who died in 40 (several recensions circulated under his name, of which one was divided into the seven groups of surahs; at the time of Uthmân, recensions attributed to Ali had authority in Damascus and seemed to have survived until the end of the fourth century); Ubayy ibn Ka'b, who died in 23, was (like Ali), one of the Prophet's secretaries; Abdallah ibn Mas'ûd, who died in 30, a former shepherd and early convert and faithful companion to the Prophet, had a perfect oral knowledge of the Koran. His corpus did not contain the *Fâtiha* and the two last verses of the actual Koran.[5]

Unfortunately, toward the fourth century of the Hijra, no trace was left of any of these works. Only those of Abû Bakr, Ubayy, Alî, and Ibn Mas'ûd are known to us, and then only through certain details reported by authors from the first centuries of Islam. These descriptions bear on certain variants, but especially on the order of surahs, which were quite different from one corpus to another, even if they respected more or less strictly the decreasing order of length. Blachère has drawn up a comparative chart of the order adopted for certain surahs in the corpus of Ubayy, of Ibn Mas'ûd, and of our vulgate. The divergences among these works are rather significant as regards the order of surahs. Groups of surahs bearing the same mysterious letters are associated with each other in the vulgate, very little so in Ibn Mas'ûd's, and not at all in Ubayy's.[6]

These divergences in the order of surahs, depending on which corpus was being used, show that the order of our vulgate is only one among others, and that it could only have triumphed for external reasons and in obscure circumstances. Still, the descriptions of the works that have come down lead us to think that the texts of surahs that are mentioned are almost identical, except for a few variants. There is cause to wonder about this uniformity and about the date when it was realized. For, apart from the first reason advanced by Tradition about Uthmân's reform, specifically with regard to divergences in the recitation, there exists another explanation, whereby Uthmân during a prayer is said to have asked his subjects to return to him the Koranic texts they possessed in order to put together a vulgate.[7] In other words, according to this account the surahs were not yet constituted and ratified in their content in Uthmân's time, outside of the ones that had been widely known during Muhammad's lifetime.

Moreover, the motive attributed to Uthmân's reform initiative—to compensate for the divergences in readings—does not correspond to the avenue that he took to achieve this. In effect, he constituted a commission charged with executing copies on the basis of Abû Bakr's recension, which were to be distributed to the four corners of the empire. This solution would be comprehensible if Arabic writings at the time of Uthmân were not seriously deficient, especially from a vocal standpoint. In these conditions, everything leads us to believe that the thesis of a written Uthmânian recension designed to serve as a reference document was forged at a time when Arabic writing was vocalized, that is to say, starting with the reign of the Umeyyad caliph Abd al-Malîk (685–705 CE).

THE DIFFICULTIES OF THE WRITING

Yet even here, the history of the reform of Arabic writing remains uncertain. The invention of vowels has been mistakenly attributed to the poet of Bassora, Abû al-Aswad al-Du'ali (died in 69 H/688 CE). Another story tells us that a governor of Iraq, Ubayd Allah ibn Ziyâd (died in 67 H/686 CE), asked his scribes to introduce a sign for the long vowels, thereby permitting a distinction, for example, between *qâla* (he said) and *qul!* (say!). His successor, the famous al-Hajjâj, during the reign of Caliph Abd al-Mâlik is said to have ordered Nasr ibn ʿÂṣim (died in 89 H/707 CE) to introduce vocalic and diacritical signs into the Koran. Another story attributes to Yahya ibn Yaʿmur al-Laythî (died in 129 H/746 CE), celebrated reader of Bassora, the introduction of inflected vowel points during the era of al-Hajjâj.

On this subject, Blachère notes that the reform of Arabic writing took place without overall planning, and that "begun under Abd al-Mâlik, it would develop over several generations and would not be completed until the end of the 3rd or 4th centuries. How far we are from that marvelous stroke of the wand that, according to certain Muslim informants, has the whole system spring from the brain of the poet Abû al-Aswad al-Du'ali!"[8] The reform took place in two stages. First, the three short vowels (a, i, u) were notated in the most ancient manuscripts by points in different colors or in different positions (above, below, or alongside consonants). Then later, diacritical signs were introduced to distinguish consonants with the same graphic, to mark doubled consonants, and lastly, to signpost recitation aloud.

This observation certainly pertains to the history of the shaping of Koranic texts, which could not have prevailed more than very gradually. Unfortunately, the paleographic data are of no help to us, for the Koranic manuscripts in our possession in only extremely rare cases go back beyond the second century of the Hijra. Grohmann notes (according to E. Herzfeld, cited in the *Ephemerides Orientales O. Harrassovitz* of January 28, 1928) the existence, among the Persian collections, of a Koranic manuscript bearing the date 94 H/712 CE, which corresponds with the reign of Walîd I (705–715 CE), successor to Abd al-Mâlik. Herzfeld also signals two other copies dated 102 and 107.[9] If these mentions were authentic, we would have here the most ancient Koranic manuscripts that are dated. They might in fact correspond to manuscripts in "Hedjazian" writing in the Bibliothèque Nationale de Paris (BNP no. 326). The manuscripts discovered in the Great Mosque of Sanaa in 1972 remain still more difficult to date, as admitted by Count von Bothmer, one of the specialists who has studied them. Only one fragment among the twelve thousand that were found bears a date: "Ramadan 357/August 968,"[10] which is far from resolving the problem of dating the oldest fragments.

In summary, at the present time there remains no trace of the state of the Koran as it existed before the end of the first century of the Hijra, or a little later, which brings us back to the reign of Walîd ibn Abd al-Mâlik (705–715), the era of the last shaping of the Koran attributed to the governor of Iraq, al-Hajjâj.

Lacking the ancient manuscripts of the first century of the Hijra, the historian must be content with the testimony that has come down to us. But here again, a new disappointment awaits us, for practically all the works that flourished shortly before the end of the Umayyad dynasty dealing with the differences between the compendiums (*ikhtilâf al-masâhif*) of the Koran have in fact disappeared. These were comparative studies of the state of the Koranic text as it was practiced (especially orally) in the great regions of the Muslim Empire: Arabia, Syria, and Iraq. One of the oldest books of which we know was written by Ibn Âmir al-Yaḥsubî (died in 118 H/736 CE); one of the last works on the Korans was by Ibn Ashta al-Iṣfahânî (died in 360 H/970 CE). However, only the book by Ibn Abî Dâwûd (died in 316 H/928 CE) has come down to us. Our knowledge of these works actually comes via citations that later authors inserted into either their commentaries on the Koran, into works on Koranic readings (*qirâ'ât*), or else into treatises on grammar, and so on.

In addition, Tradition has arranged things so that what has filtered down to us are only minor variants. This was admitted by a writer of the fourth century, Abû Ḥayyân: he had not cited in his work those Koranic variants that were too far removed from the "Uthmânian" text.[11] This historiographic fact is of the highest importance, if one links it to the information we do have on the persecutions suffered by all those who obstinately continued to use noncanonical variants, as was the case with Ibn Shanabûdh (245–328).

The traditionalist thesis about the Uthmânian collection is only a fantastic reconstruction, hiding a reality that people sought to erase from human memory: the Koran is multiple because its text has a history and thus presents an evolution, as well as variations over time. And this history was only possible because it was in the nature of the redaction of the text that would eventually become the Koran to take the routes of elaboration, composition, stylization, and rectification. In short, it was the product of a historical elaboration (divine or human, it does not matter), and not a dictation carried out on the basis of a pre-existing text, definitive and ready to be published. From the time of the prophecy, the divine word had to be shaped, a task that was incumbent on scribes, and it is this operation that later generations have tried to erase, in order to give a simplified and more-reassuring image of the Koranic message, that of a text composed by God in person.

THE MYTH OF "UTHMÂN"

The principal and the most decisive lesson that one should draw from the information we do have on these ancient Koranic corpuses claimed to be noncanonical is that they are essentially comparable to the text of our vulgate called "Uthmânian": the works do not contain much variation except for details, neither in their structure, their content, or in the number of surahs. For one thing, the texts in each corpus are the same from one corpus to another, with small variants. They seem (still according to the descriptions we have of them) to carry a total number of surahs that differs very marginally from the vulgate, depending on whether or not one adopts certain very short surahs, like the *Fâtiha*, or the two final surahs. The only other visible difference, without real importance anyway, is in the order of surahs, which sometimes varies significantly from one corpus to another.

From these observations, we may conclude that the ensemble of the known noncanonical works by ancient authors belong to one and the same generation, and were constituted at a well-determined stage in the evolution of revealed texts: the same one that witnessed the present constitution of both the content and the number of surahs.

There is a paradox here that will not have escaped the reader. The most ancient works in the corpuses of the Korans, like those of Ubayy and Ibn Mas'ûd, which were supposed to have been formed independently of the recension realized by the first caliphs Abû Bakr and Uthmân, all resemble the latter like two drops of water, and they therefore all belong to the same collection. This situation presents us with an alternative: either the definitive collection was realized in the time of the Prophet—but in this case, a Uthmânian recension never existed, or else this collecting took place after the death of the Prophet (in this case it could not have been realized by some companion of the Prophet like Zayd, Uthmân, Alî, Abû Bakr, Ibn Mas'ûd, Ubayy), in which case would have resulted from the slow evolution of an oral tradition relying on writings that reproduced the partial compendiums of texts revealed in the Prophet's time. This is the most likely hypothesis, considering the structure of the text that we have studied, and the oldest traces of the Koran that are still divergent.

Moreover, the definitive version of the Koran leaves no doubt about the absence of a veritable systematic and voluntary collection that would have taken place under a definite authority. When we observe the division of surahs in the Koran, we quickly see that they did not obey any criterion of composition at all. This can be well perceived in the extreme disparity that exists between the long surahs: fifty-some pages for the longest, "The Heifer," as opposed to one and a half lines for the shortest. In fact, this longest surah is the equivalent in length to the 75 last surahs combined (out of a total of 114 surahs in the Koran). It is clear that, if there had existed even a slight desire for a systematic gathering and definitive shaping of the Koranic text, then the Koran would not today present a disequilibrium so pronounced in so important a facet as that of surahs.

After about a half century, this state of affairs ended up settling, thanks to the collections composed by anonymous scribes, into a model corpus that was made official under the Umayyad caliph Abd al-Mâlik or under his son Walîd I, that is to say, perhaps in the time of al-Hajjâj's rule.

THE MANUSCRIPT OF SAMARKAND

The manuscript of Samarkand is a composite, containing portions written by different scribes at different dates. It is not complete, since dozens of pages are missing at the beginning and at the end, and some in its middle. It would assuredly merit the deeper study that we are cruelly lacking for ancient manuscripts. It is now located in Tashkent, after long peregrinations that brought it in 1485 to Samarkand, then in 1868 to St. Petersburg, ending up in 1917 in Tashkent. In 1905, Czar Nicholas II had Dr. Pissarev make fifty reproductions of it under the title "Kufic Koran of Samarkand," of which some copies can still be found in Western libraries.

There are some particularities of this manuscript that are of interest to us here.[12] It has omissions that are due, some of them, to a scribe's negligence; some have been rectified by corrections in the margins. Some variants are worth remembering. The name "Allah" is sometimes replaced in the Samarkand manuscript by the pronoun *hu* (*-wwa*), as in verses 2:284 (ms. of S. 90) and 3:78 (ms. of S. 109). Sometimes, it is omitted, as in 2:283 (ms. of S. 89) and 5:119 (ms. of S. 252). In 3:37, it is the expression "*inna Allah*" that disappears from the manuscript (p. 92), without harming the comprehension of the text. Note also the variant of verse 3:146 (ms. of S. 134) that speaks of "what [Muhammad] (*mâ asâbahu*) underwent" in the course of the battle of Uhud, whereas the vulgate speaks of "what [his companions] underwent (*mâ asâbahum*)." It seems we have in this manuscript the first version of the text that alludes to the severe wounds the Prophet received during this battle, a vulnerability that would have provoked doubts in the minds of a certain number of his companions (see verses 3:146–47).

Moreover, this manuscript gives us interesting clues concerning the history of the composition of the verses. Like the most ancient manuscripts, our manuscript does not demarcate verses in certain parts, and elsewhere only for sets of five or ten verses. These hesitations are very probably due to the fact that the manuscript is composed of fragments from different dates. But a quick comparison of the manuscript with our vulgate shows us a phenomenon worthy of interest. In three cases of verses—6:91, 6:128, and 7:25—where the vulgate signals the end of the verse by adding the conjunction *wa* (and) at the start of the following verse, this is absent in our manuscript. On the other hand, we find an inverse case (3:113), where it is the vulgate that suppresses the *wa* at the start of the verse, although it is part of the phrase in the manuscript. We also find some of the Seven "Readings" also omitting the *wa* at the start of certain verses, contrary to the vulgate. This relation between the presence and absence of the sign of the end of the verse and of the coordinating conjunction would merit a study that would shed more light on the history of how the Koranic texts came to be enduringly divided into verses. But we may deduce from the preceding that this division of the text into verses necessitated a readjustment of the text to adapt it better to its new recitatory dynamic.

THE MYTH OF AUTHENTICITY

Can Muslim orthodoxy continue to claim a literal and compositional authenticity for the Koran? The Koran itself, as we have seen, invalidates such a claim. Koranic doctrine in this respect is quite clear: the divine message has no single form but corresponds to two distinct realities, the original and the copy. The original is designated in the Koran by the precise term *kitâb*, and this writing was consigned to a heavenly tablet (*lawh*), well guarded by and near to God. As for the copy, it is an emanation and an extract from this original and results from a chain of transmitting agents: Gabriel, Muhammad, and the scribes, as well as secretaries assigned to the shaping of the revealed statements. Above all, we have seen that it was by an act of inspiration (*wahy*) that the passage of the *kitâb* to the *qur'ân* was realized, and not by a simple reproduction of a text.

At no time has the Koran claimed a literal identity between the revealed text and its divine source. This is so evident that even the two myths imagined by orthodoxy in order to prove the authenticity of the Koran remain scarcely convincing. It was effectively claimed that the archangel Gabriel had adopted the habit, every year during the month of Ramadan, of taking stock of the revealed text: correcting it, putting into order the verses revealed during the preceding year, and also eliminating verses said to be abrogated. In short, here we have work of a scribal nature that people have attempted to impute to a divine authority in order to legitimate it. The other myth attributed the communication of the revealed text to two successive stages: first, the text of the Koran came down in its entirety by traversing the seven heavens; arriving at the lowest heaven, it remained there, conserved in a place called *beit al-ʿizza*. Second, from there, Gabriel drew verses that he communicated regularly to the Prophet during the whole period of Koranic revelation, meaning over more than twenty years. It is clear that this latter myth invented by Muslim orthodoxy also tries to blot out the contingent character of the revealed texts, which relates to the fact that they are manifestly linked to the long history of the Prophet and to the vicissitudes of his struggle against the Qurayshites.

THE SCRIBAL FUNCTION

In reality, the changing character of Koranic verses, in their literal meaning or in their very existence—for God reserves the right to change and even abrogate verses (2:106)—does not necessarily put into question their conformity with the original, inasmuch as the revealed text becomes necessarily different from its inspirational source, since what matters is respect for its spirit alone, not for its letter. So the issue is the habitual practices proper to the work of scribes dedicated to the shaping of the divine words. No doubt this work is of the same nature as that performed by "the heavenly scribes" who have in hand the "honored pages" (80:13–15) of the heavenly tablet.

We are in the presence of an ancient and constant Oriental practice that always confides the writing of contracts, correspondence, and literary works (versified or not) to specialists in writing. And this is not only an issue of writing technique, but also of the composition and literary editing of thought according to a style and a phraseology that are both codified. Therefore this scribal function was attributed to a tutelary divinity like Nabû among the Mesopotamians, or Thôt among the Egyptians, or al-Kutba among the Nabuteans.[13]

In one sense, the scribe was "inspired" by the author whose thinking the scribe was reconstructing or even interpreting. The same was true of the prophets and kings whose literary or legal writing was directly inspired by each's tutelary divinity. Ancient reformers like Urukagina of the Mesopotamian town of Larsa 4,500 years ago, or

Hammurabi 3,700 years ago, had edited legal codes so as to "restore the Law of God," the former inspired by the god Ningirsu, the latter by the god Shamash. Here, as in the Koran, the key word is "*wa<u>h</u>y*," or "inspiration," not a word-by-word dictation. The celestial *kitâb* as consigned to tablets was first communicated to Gabriel, who inspired it in Muhammad, so that he in turn could communicate it to his scribes charged with putting it into literal form to serve as *qur'ân* and as liturgical recitation.

In this sense, biblical tradition did not proceed otherwise. When God asked Jeremiah to put into writing the revelations he had received from him, the Prophet charged the scribe Baruch with writing under his dictation the divine words (Jeremiah 36:1–4). Sometimes, the prophet was charged not only with writing down "a vision" but also of explaining it, as with Habakkuk: "Write the vision and make it plain on tablets so that a runner may read it" (Habakkuk 2:1–2 NRSV). This form of transmission of divine will by means of a vision corresponds with the *âya* or Koranic sign that God transmits to his Prophet, in which the inspired word is called on to take form according to the customary usages of the elaboration of sacred texts to serve for recitation/*qur'ân*. Thus, the prophetic technique of Muhammad scarcely differs from that of his biblical homologues, who had hardly any more concern for the literal nature of the inspired statements. Here, fidelity to the message is not reduced to a literal conformity to an original, but only to a respect for its spirit.

STEREOTYPES AND PHRASEOLOGY

This issue of the literal nature of revelation no longer makes sense as soon as the prophetic discourse is subjected to the rhetorical and phraseological norms to which it was asked to conform. John Wansbrough has analyzed the schemas of revelation that served as models for the composition of the Koranic sentence, and that gave it its incomparable stylistic specificity. There are, then, rhetorical conven-

tions that mark the prophetic discourse and that one may easily identify thanks to the introductory formulas (see the preambles studied
above) and the concluding ones, which vary according to the topic of
the discourse, such as rewards, signs, exile, the treaty, to mention only
some of the themes studied by Wansbrough.[14]

It is clear that the preponderance of rhetorical formulas—with
their syntactical particularities—constitutes a fundamental element in
the identification of the particular and incomparable style of the
Koran. It is even quite probable that we are in the presence of a scribal
school that would have perfected over generations this type of rhetoric
and would have contributed to shaping the Koranic discourse, on the
basis of the revelations brought by Muhammad—unless he himself
was a member of such a body, with which he might have continued to
collaborate (or not) during his apostolate.

THE PRACTICE OF RECOMPOSITION

Wansbrough has studied the variants of the Koranic story about the
Arab prophet Shu'ayb in three surahs: 7:85–93, 11:84–95, and
26:176–90.[15] The author concludes that these various compositions of
a single story might be imputed to different authors. (Certainly the
variants of a single story are intriguing solely by their existence as
duplicates.) But it remains to be determined if the variations between
these versions really suggest Wansbrough's conclusion. The fact that
the three stories have rigorously kept the same overall plan might in
effect lead us to think that what we have here are models realized by
different people on the basis of a single template. This was an old Oriental practice, like the one touching on the story of the Flood, or the
cycle about Adam and Eve in biblical tradition, which gave rise to the
genre of the *haggadah*. Similarly one might consider that this biblical
tradition is itself an interpretation and a recomposition of ancient tales
out of Oriental antiquity.[16] This interpretative practice also bears the
name *kabbalah*, or else *midrash*, from the root word *dârash* (to

seek).[17] Here the framework of the story is conserved, but different meanings are attributed to it.

Muslim Tradition has merely followed this movement with the "*tafsîr*," the Koranic commentaries. Even the *hadîth* or prophetic sayings belong to the same genre of Koranic interpretation. This is the meaning of the Koranic function of *taṣdîq* ("*muṣaddiqan*") that any prophet accomplishes in relation to his precursors: a fidelity that does not exclude difference. The same is true of the Christian doctrine that considers that the New Testament is the "accomplishment" of the Old.

It is perhaps to this interpretative genre that the Koran is alluding when it lays claim to the genre of *mathânî*, which Muslim Tradition has identified rightly with stories. The Koran contrasts this genre with that of *muḥkam,* identified with the Law. We find here again the two biblical poles of the *haggadah* and the *halakah,* one complementing the other.

It is important to realize that the production of the Koran partook of this phenomenon of the *haggadah* throughout the twenty years of the Muhammadan revelation, hence the repetitive and composite character that emanates from this whole work. But it is quite probable also that work on the text was pursued after the death the Prophet, which then could not, in the eyes of the redactors, amount to an act of *taḥrîf* (confection of a falsehood), for they were only extending work carried out during Muhammad's lifetime.

AL-QUR'ÂN, A SCRIBAL WORK

The composition of phrases is part of the scribal institution and it constitutes an indispensable complement to revelation. The pair "prophet-and-scribe" is the usual original framework of Oriental scriptural practice: each fulfills his function and the product of their collaboration is all the more authentic as a result. If the Prophet is the mouth of God, the scribe is the pen of the Prophet. The scribe is master of the technique of the word, and like any technician, he is inspired by God. The risk inherent in this institution is quite evidently *the false*, occurring when the scribe breaks with his source.

Such is the sempiternal accusation launched back and forth among rival scribal schools. The polemic reported by Muslim Tradition on the subject of "readings" or codices called pre-Uthmânian is one remarkable illustration of this. Before the proliferation of scribal schools, one had to choose: either decide on a single "reading" and declare all the others henceforth false—and thus literal authenticity becomes the product of political consecration, itself of course "inspired." Or else take the alternative solution of declaring all schools authentic and integrating them into the canon. Such was the fate of the Koran in its primitive phase, if one accepts the idea of multiple oral and written sources developed during the lifetime of the Prophet and well afterward.[18]

But there exists another phenomenon that necessitated scribal interventions: this was the change in political attitude after the evolution in power relations between the Prophet and his enemies, whether Quraysh or biblical. Notably this involved an incessant reinterpretation of history and a revision in attitudes. It is just as difficult to believe that the first Koranic texts would not mention the accusations made against certain personages who were enemies of the Prophet and then later converted to the new faith. The fact that the Koran has kept traces of compromising denunciations is far from constituting proof that we have the totality of these denunciations.

Chapter 4

MYTHS AND PREJUDICES

I t is clear that the dominant representation that we have today of the nature and identity of the Koranic text (as of its history) is largely a product of orthodox Muslim doctrine. It has succeeded in imposing a simplistic vision of the Koranic œuvre, as well as covering up the real processes of its production and its transmission.

We can detect several dogmas about, and mythical reconstructions of, the history of the Koranic text that have contributed to this simplification: the notion of the originality of the Koran; the identification of Koranic revelation with the archetype contained in the celestial tablet; the literal revelation; the collection of the Koran as attributed to Muhammad and/or the first caliphs; the divine preservation of the Koranic text in the course of its transmission from generation to generation; the absolute trustworthiness of oral and written transmission; and finally, the myth of the inimitability of the Koranic discourse.

THE MYTH OF ORIGINALITY

Among the prejudices that fashion the consciousness that Muslim orthodoxy has of the Koran is the notion of an original text bringing forth ideas and information that are unprecedented since the beginning of time. This popular prejudice belongs to a movement of apologetics that has touched everything related to the apostolate of Muhammad, with no concern to respect either the letter or the spirit of the Koran. Thus the language of the Koran is considered to be the most perfect there can be—vis-à-vis all other human languages, or even other kinds of Arab speech. Nevertheless, Koranic language is sometimes far from respecting the most elementary rules of grammar or style. Muslim Tradition has detected a certain number of faulty uses, on which it has lavished a treasury of ingenuity in order to justify them. Any borrowing from foreign lexicons is admitted only with difficulty, for Muslim doctrine has taken literally the Koranic assertion of the perfect Arabic-ness of the language of the Koran, and it has seen in any foreign terminology a denial of this assertion.

In addition, any application of the critical historical method to religious stories was considered out of place. Doctrine has been suspicious of parallels that might be drawn with the Bible, not to mention possible correlations with legal and religious texts of Oriental antiquity. In doing so, orthodoxy ignores that it is openly impeding Koranic doctrine, which has claimed high and loud its fidelity to stories reported in revealed books. Generally speaking, biblical texts are ignored by Muslims. The Bible is in fact censured; it is not admitted into homes, and still less into mosques.

The pretext invoked to justify this situation is the alteration that is thought to have affected the Bible in the long course of its transmission. However, the developments that we have just reviewed regarding the obstacles that really precluded a faithful transmission of the Koranic text invite a much greater indulgence toward the biblical text.

We can only regret this distrust on the part of Muslim doctrine toward the Bible, even if the sentiment is sometimes reciprocal. Some

Koranic passages find their explanation or their source of inspiration in the biblical text. Let us cite a concrete case recently discovered by a monk, Lucien-Jean Bord, regarding the source of inspiration for the *Fâtiha*, or "The Opening," the surah that opens the Book of the Koran.[1] Brother Bord has shown the astonishing affinity of the first Koranic text with the first psalm of the Bible. Here it is in the New International Version: "1) Blessed is the man who does not walk in the counsel of the wicked or stand in the way of sinners or sit in the seat of mockers. 2) But his delight is in the law of the Lord, and on his law he meditates day and night. 3) He is like a tree planted by streams of water, which yields its fruit in season and whose leaf does not wither. Whatever he does prospers. 4) Not so the wicked! They are like chaff that the wind blows away. 5) Therefore the wicked will not stand in the judgment, nor sinners in the assembly of the righteous. 6) For the Lord watches over the way of the righteous, but the way of the wicked will perish." And now here is the *Fâtiha*, in Dawood's translation for Penguin: "Praise be to God, Lord of the Universe, the Compassionate, the Merciful, Sovereign of the Day of Judgment! You alone we worship, and to You alone we turn for help. Guide us to the straight path, the path of those whom You have favored, not of those who have incurred Your wrath, nor of those who have gone astray." One immediately sees the similarity of the two texts, especially regarding the essential theme contrasting the path of the righteous with the path of the sinners, with the idea of the Day of Judgment in the background.[2]

This comparison between the two texts is certainly not due to chance, for the Koran has given the theme of the psalm a choice place. First, in the Koran the term "psalm" (*zabûr*) is relatively more frequent than the one that designates the essential text of the Torah (nine, as opposed to eighteen for the latter). Second, the Koran considers that the text revealed to Muhammad was already existing "in the *psalms* of the ancients" (26:196), an allusion to biblical writings.

We may provide another justification for the intuition of Brother Bord when the Koran returns to the theme treated in verses 3 and 4 of the same first psalm that inspired the *Fâtiha*: "3) [He] is like a tree planted by streams of water, which yields its fruit in season and whose leaf does not wither. Whatever he does prospers. 4) Not so the wicked! They are like chaff that the wind blows away." The Koran reprises the same parable: "Do you not see how God had given this parable: a good word is like a good tree, whose root is firm and its branches are in the sky; it yields its fruits in every season. . . . But an evil word is like an evil tree torn out of the earth and shorn of all its roots. God will strengthen the faithful with His steadfast Word, both in this life and in the life to come. He leads the wrongdoers astray. God accomplishes what He pleases" (14:24–27). It is unnecessary to insist here on a striking similarity between the two parables, down to the details. This last Koranic verse takes up the theme of straying (_dalla_) that we find mentioned at the end of the _Fâtiha_—an additional support for the hypothesis of a redactional link between the latter and the first psalm.

But it is not only biblical literature that furnished redactional elements to the Koran. Let us mention here the discovery made by Isidore Lévy[3] of the affinity that exists between the Koranic story of the legend of the Seven Sleepers[4] and the story of the end of Pândavas in the next to last episode of the Hindu epic _Mahabharata_.[5] Jean Lambert, who has compared these two stories in more detail, has highlighted their astonishing similarity.[6] It is likely this epic Indian story was transmitted through Persia, only later to find itself in the hands of Arab scribal circles.

FROM THE _KITÂB_ TO THE _QUR'ÂN_

It is on the theological level that the Koran brings the clearest denial of the myth of the literal "authenticity" of the revealed text, since, as we have seen, the revealed text is presented as a product derived from an original preserved on a heavenly tablet; thus it is not the authentic text. Between the two, there is the work of the prophetic and scribal transmitters who were charged with putting the text at the disposal of humans. Humankind does not receive the divine message contained in the *kitâb* except in the form of the *qur'ân*, that is to say, in the form of a liturgical lesson or recitation. The authenticity of the Koran does not reside in its identity with the original, but only in the fact that it is a discourse inspired in an authentic messenger.

In effect, the nature of the prophetic function shows us that the message to be transmitted is only rarely a solemn announcement or a declaration of principles, the sort of thing that would legitimately find a place in a heavenly tablet. In fact, the transmitted material often concerns particular affairs, issues often relating to situations that are contingent and specific to the Prophet or to the community. In short, Koranic discourse is essentially engaged—politically, polemically, and pedagogically—but it is only very marginally normative in the sense that it enunciates norms or laws that must be respected and that refer back to an original text, as is the case with the Mosaic law inscribed on the stone tablets. In fact, the conserved heavenly tablet constitutes a guarantee of the authenticity of the prophetic apostolate and of the *spirit* of the message to be transmitted, but not of its *letter*. This is what allows God to change—or to abrogate—the oracular signs transmitted by the Prophet without thereby betraying the heavenly tablet.

It is clear, in these conditions, that the words revealed to Muhammad are not the result of some dictation of the original words, but of a more complex process of *wahy*, or "inspiration." Arthur Jeffery has studied the nature of this phenomenon through the two most technically important Koranic terms, *tanzîl* (descent) and *wahy*, which are in practice interchangeable.[7] The notion of *tanzîl* was current in the ancient Orient as it was in the biblical world, designating the mode of transmitting or moving the spirit of revelation from on high to down below. The word *wahy*, which is found in the Ethiopian term *wahâya*, signifies precisely "to indicate, to set in motion, to push, to incite, to inspire." The idea of dictation is absent from the Koran and from ancient or biblical cultures. Generally, it is a spirit "inspired" (42:52) in the Prophet that "reveals" a discourse to him—of course, the best one that can be conceived.

In a previous book, I have given the example of the Babylonian poem "Erra/Nergal," where a scribe named Kabti-ilâni-Marduk plays the prophetic role of an inspired person who, having had a vision in the night, was able to "compose" a poem under the inspiration of the god Ishum to honor the god Erra. Ishum is the equivalent of the archangel Gabriel, since he is the inspirational spirit delegated by his tutelary god Erra. Kabti-ilâni-Marduk tells us that as soon as he awoke, he "composed" the poem in such a way that he "omitted nothing of it, nor added a single line!"[8] We see here the duality of the act of revealed writing: a text written by a scribe who knew it by means of inspiration and who, in order to justify the divine character of this "composition," attributes its merit to the inspiring genius down to each comma.

The Koran obeys this way of transmitting revelation, but without making the claim for a literal fidelity—a claim that arises more from apologetics than from the realm of historical truth. What is important is that the text is revealed, never dictated, and done so through a chain of transmitters that ends with the scribe, who takes on the "composition" of the text and its shaping into form. This is the function assumed by the "secretaries" of Muhammad who were responsible for the redaction of the Koran.

Of course, the Tradition that gives us information about these scribes has worked hard to make us believe that they merely wrote under the Prophet's dictation. And so it nabs some *dishonest* secretaries who took malicious pleasure in writing according to their own inspiration: we are told that when they die, the earth refuses to receive them. In fact, these edifying stories, associated with the thesis clearly admitted by Tradition of a revelation according to the spirit and not according to the letter, are probably reconstructions of older stories that did acknowledge the active and normalized role of scribes in the "composition" of the Koran. These scribes were primarily entrusted with elaborating a style in accordance with the genre of the oracle, with its preambles and closing and doxological formulas. They also had to identify other genres, such as stories, parables, legal stipulations, prayers, glorification of the divine, and so on, by employing particular stylistic norms drawn in part from sectarian religious communities.

Moreover, the Koran makes an allusion to this milieu when it speaks of the reproach made by miscreants who say: "This is but a forgery of his own invention, in which others have helped him. . . . Fables of the ancients he has written: they are dictated to him morning and evening!" (25:4–5). But curiously, the Koran does not defend itself against this accusation, as if it acknowledged these miscreants without sharing the conclusions that they want to draw. We know from Tradition that one of the secretaries of Muhammad, Zayd ibn Thâbit, knew Syriac and no doubt had access to the religious literature of Judeo-Christian or Manichean sects. So here he reproaches Muhammad for having recruited secretaries whose usual function was not only to put the words into writing, but also to shape the text that had been entrusted to them, according to a technique specific to the scribe's job.

In any case, what springs out of the study of the structure of Koranic discourse is its stereotypical aspects, both in rhyme and in repetitiveness, which suggests its oral vocation as a *qur'ân* or recitation.[9]

We are undoubtedly confronted by a text that is the product of a long effort of elaboration in both its content and its form. But whether this effort was performed by Muhammad alone, or, more probably, with the help of scribes, is a matter of secondary importance: what is important is that the Koranic text offers us a remarkable example of a particular literary genre, in which one may identify and list the techniques used to produce it, and of which one may also determine the evolution throughout the revelation. Then in a second stage, one might compare these techniques with those that were known in Muhammad's time from the writings of Judeo-Christian sects. One might also usefully extend this inquiry to ancient Oriental civilizations, which first perfected a religious and literary rhetoric that one rediscovers in Arab culture.

THE MYTH OF THE COLLECTION

After the myth of the literalness of revelation, we come to the myth of the *jamʿ*, or the collection of Koranic texts into a structured book. This is the second proof offered by Muslim orthodoxy to give credit to the idea of an original text that was entirely and authentically divine. We have already observed that the extreme inequality in length between long surahs and short ones, the total absence of an overall plan for the book and especially for the surahs—all prove incontestably that there was not in Muhammad's lifetime, nor after it, a desire to harmonize the multifarious revealed units contained within a synthetic entity called the Koran, or the *Mushaf*.

This scriptural entity is veritably mythic in the sense that there does not exist a single Koranic "composition" but several revelations without links between them, and that they were not designed to make up a book. In this regard, let us recall that Uthmân was reproached for having reduced the Koran to a single book: "The *qur'ân* was in the form of [several] writings, and you have reduced them into a single one (*kâna al-qur'ânu kutuban fa-taraktahâ illâ wâhidan*)."[10] We also remember the reluctance attributed to Zayd when the project to collect the Koran was proposed to him. All of this shows the incongruous character of the idea of a Koran, even in the eyes of Tradition, which in this echoes the debates at the time when a Koranic canon was being made official.

When did this canonization take place? Here the paleographic information hardly helps us, since the most ancient known manuscripts do not go back further than the end of the first or end of the second century of the Hijra. No doubt it was in the Umeyyad era that a decision was made to constitute not a book but only a compendium of various sheets (*suhufs*) put into order according to length and then numbered. So it was a matter more of an official inventory of revealed texts such as they had reached that generation. In order to legitimate such an enterprise, this operation was variously said to be attributed to the third caliph, Uthmân, sometimes to Abû Bakr, and even to Muhammad. But this book never received a definitive title, for the

Koran did not give one to itself, for the simple reason that the idea of a book was never raised until after the death of the Prophet.

THE MYTH OF PERFECT TRANSMISSION

Tradition has insisted upon the idea of an impeccable transmission of the Koranic text from its revelation right down to our day, to prove that the text we possess is well and truly the one of the heavenly tablet that God has preserved from any alteration. It is sufficient to recall the variants that Muslim orthodoxy has itself recognized and even codified under the appellation of *qirâ'ât* (readings), or *ikhtilâfât* (divergences), in order to reduce this pious pretension to naught. Variations began within the very framework of revelation, since the Koran established the principle of abrogation (*naskh*).

Moreover, Arabic writing of the period was deficient, deprived of diacritical signs and vocalic signs until a very late date, somewhere between the end of the Umeyyad dynasty and the fourth century of the Hijra. To respond to this objection, people have vaunted the phenomenal capacity of the ancient Arabs to memorize texts and to preserve them from any error. Again, this is a myth that a great authority, Ibn Mujâhid (245–324 H), unwittingly undermined when he wanted to explain why there were Koranic variants. He says in his introduction to his *Book of the Seven Readings* (*Kitâb al-sabᶜ fî al-qirâ'ât*) that it might happen that someone who has memorized the Koran "forgets, and loses what he had received, and he recites the text without discernment. And so he reads it in an arbitrary manner, which leads him, in order to defend his innocence, to attribute this new reading to another reader. And if he is found to be a trustworthy man, then people imitate him. Also, if he happens to forget and to commit an error in good faith, he then sticks firmly to it, and requires it of others." As we see, this testimony about the first Muslim generations refutes definitively the myth of the infallibility of the memory of those reciting the Koran in order to conserve it.

But it is not only memories that give out; scribes are just as fallible as those who recite from memory. Rare are the Koranic manuscripts that have come down to us that are free of errors of transcription. The famous manuscript of Samarkand well illustrates the real risk of errors that may affect the writing, due solely to the fact of there being scribes.

Let us recall here a curious story related by Muslim Tradition concerning an accidental destruction of the Koran by fire during the time of the revelation. Tabarânî relates this saying from Muhammad: "If the Koran had been put into leather, the fire would not have consumed it [*law kâna al-qurân fî jild mâ 'akalathu al-nâr*]." A similar *hadîth* has been related by Ibn Hanbal: "If one puts the Koran into leather and if one throws it on the fire, the Koran will not burn." Still more intriguing is yet another *hadîth* from Muhammad reported by 'Iṣmat ibn Mâlik: "If they had collected the Koran in leather (*ihâb*), Allâh would not have made it consumed by the fire [*mâ 'aḥraqahu allâhu bi al-nâr*]." What is the mystery behind this destruction of the Koran by fire? Was the Koran partially burned during Muhammad's lifetime? Does this destruction have some relation with the destruction attributed to Uthmân of the noncanonical texts of the Koran? Nothing today allows us to go any further with these speculations. But the story is worth remembering in the context of the history of the Koran and of its transmission, which, as we have seen, has been much more fragile than we are led to think by the dogma falsely attributed to the Koran, according to which God was engaged in safeguarding it (*innâ lahû la-ḥâfidhûn*), whereas it was the heavenly tablet that was the object of divine care, not the revealed text.

THE MYTH OF INIMITABILITY

The Koran affirms it categorically: "If humans and djinns combined to produce a *qur'ân* identical with this one, they could not do so, even though they helped one another as best they could" (17:88). However, this declaration about the inimitability of the revealed text should not be taken literally, for it belongs to a genre that glorifies divine works. Since God is superior to his living creatures, so then everything they are capable of producing could not equal the work of their creator. And so it would be mistaken to draw from any affirmation of the excellence of the Koranic text an argument for its inimitable character. No more so than from elsewhere, when it is said that "if the Koran had not come from God, they [the Impious] could surely have found in it many contradictions [*ikhtilâf*]" (4:82). In fact, the Koran does contain numerous contradictions, which Muslim Tradition has tried to resolve, notably by resorting to the doctrine of abrogation—just as the Koranic theory of ambiguous verses (*mutashâbih*) takes the opposite view in order to assert the absence of contradiction.

However, an admission of contradiction does not in principle prejudge the contribution of human beings to works that are divinely inspired. In fact, the principle of excellence might be equally applied just as much to *kâhins* (soothsayers) and to poets. This claim might simply relate to the status of any revealed work: either it must be the product of God's exclusive contribution, or else agents participate but are responsible for its technical realization, like prophets or scribes, which does not put into question the divine nature of a realization that keeps intact its attribute of excellence. For example, when God granted a favor to Solomon, he had some djinns construct his palace. These djinns were under God's direct supervision (34:12), and they achieved a work that still merits the status of excellence and incomparability, and so on. In short, God often utilizes external agents in the realization of his works, and this does not affect the latter's excellence, or even their divine character, since technically they are the product of a divine *waḥy* that is applied regardless to produce something, either speech or objects. Thus the production of the Koran was confided successively to heavenly agents (such as Gabriel) and then to terrestrial ones (Muhammad and his scribes), all acting through divine inspiration.

AUTHENTICITY OF THE *WAHY*

Quite another question is the authenticity of the *wahy*, which should not be confused with the question of the literal authenticity of the text produced through revelation. The authenticity of the *wahy* gave rise to an intense debate throughout Muhammad's period of prophecy. He was accused of having benefited from the teaching of certain Judeo-Christian sectarians with whom he was in contact. The Koran has explicitly recognized these contacts: "We know that they [unbelievers] say: 'The one who inspires it [*yu'allimuhu*] is only mortal.' But the tongue of the man to whom they allude is a pagan, while this is eloquent Arabic speech" (16:103). "Those who do not believe have said: 'This is but a forgery of his own invention, in which others have helped him.'. . . And they say: 'Fables of the ancients he has written: they are dictated to him morning and evening!'" (25:4–5).

Tradition has generously given us details of these informants, starting with Tabarî and many others.[11] The Koran has not been able to defend itself against such attacks, since their pertinence was recognized, so that Tradition could not accuse them of lying, though it tried to sketch (without great conviction) an argument turning on the difference in language between the Prophet and the said informants. The only serious and "ritual" response was to recall the omnipotence and omniscience of the divine.

The question of "informants" of Muhammad has undoubtedly been confused with that of Christian scribes assigned to the redaction and composition of the text. Tradition has recognized their "fraudulent" participation in correcting the concluding formulas of the revealed texts.[12] In my opinion, this is only an adaptation of an original fact: the role, normally assumed in the elaboration of the Koranic text, by scribes, which was reduced by the new Muslim ideology to a minor role; in cases of "variants," the scribes or informants were suspected of falsification.

Gilliot has detected a remarkable common trait in this class of "informants": their exercise of metallurgical skills, designated by the technical term *qayn*. Coming from a Hebrew, Syriac, and Ethiopian root, this term refers to "the action of singing, launching into a funerary lamentation [*qayn/qayna*]."[13] Gilliot suggests we should connect this skill with metal to a form of initiatory culture, like that practiced in Indo-European lands. In my opinion, things could be even simpler: the link between metalworking and singing owes much to the very technique of work with metal, which demands a certain "rhythm." The cadence of metalworking must have been accompanied by songs, in line with an ancient practice that survives even today; the exercise of certain skills is often enlivened by working songs. We find a remarkable example in the Arabic musical genre of the "*mawwâl*," whose origin would have been a sung accompaniment to the rhythmic march of the camel in the desert.

It could have been the same for our blacksmiths associated with the singing genre of the *qayn*. That Muhammad's "informants" might have been blacksmiths, in these conditions, is a very interesting indication of their possible contribution, as scribes, to the elaboration of the Koranic style, from the work of its rhythm and of its conventional formulas, since these masters of metal were also normally masters of versification and of style.

What is important here for us is the argument raised against these informants-scribes concerning the veracity of the source of the inspiration, not the divine authenticity of the production of the Koranic text. We should not forget that the principal stake that dominated the period of prophetic revelation was to prove that the prophetic mission claimed by Muhammad was indeed authentic, and not to prove the literal authenticity of the divine message. It was not until well after the death of the Prophet that there was a change of perspective, at a time when it was no longer necessary to establish the authenticity of the prophetic apostolate. But given that prophecy broke down with the demise of Muhammad, the revealed text became the sole source of legitimacy and theological reference for Muslims, as it was for the secular powers at the time. And as this unique source of reference, the Koranic text henceforth acquired a new sacredness, the one enjoyed until then by the heavenly original, the preserved tablet. Therefore the religious dispute completely changed direction, and emergent Islam had to create from scratch a new dogma about the literal authenticity of the revealed text and to invent the myth of the annual correction of the revealed text by Muhammad with his inspiring archangel Gabriel.

CONCLUSION

At the end of this journey, I hope to have demonstrated the complexity of our questioning of the authenticity of the Koranic text.

What is important to know and to discover in this domain is not so much the alterations that affected the Koranic text in the course of its revelation or afterward, than the religious world as it was represented at the time of the revelation. This world had its own vision of the divine that is no longer our own. It also had its own way of seeing God, of communicating with humans, and its own representation of the prophets—all of which are hard to imagine in our own day.

The God of the Koran, Allah, would certainly not recognize himself in the idea that we have of him today, fourteen centuries after the Koranic revelation. In fact, God is far from being a disincarnate being, abstract and absolute, as he is represented today. Reading the Koran, he rather resembles the God of Abraham and of the Bible: a living God, who is of course wise, but who also has moments of anger, and has preferences, desires, and needs. He is a God in the image of Oriental monarchs: a God who surpasses all humans, of course, but a being with a human resemblance.

The same is true of his prophets, who have been so idealized in our day that they have been turned into divine beings. Even their companions have become the object of an almost divine cult; Muslim Tradition has compared them to "the stars of Heaven."

It is remarkable that the traditionalist biographies of Muhammad have effaced practically any testimony and all information on his life before he was forty years old, that is to say, before the start of his apostolate. In the Muslim consciousness, Muhammad was born an accomplished prophet, and from his birth, all he had to do was wait sagely for the hour of his mission. For example, Ibn Hazm (994–1064 CE) asserts that "we know with certainty that God has preserved His Prophets from adultery and from being the sons of adultery. . . . We know with certitude that Allah immunized them before their apostolate from anything they could be reproached for in the course of their apostolate, such as theft, aggression, harshness, pederasty, fornication, prejudices against people regarding their wives, their goods, or their persons." Then, Ibn Hazm reports a story attributed to Hassan, son of Ali ibn Abî Tâlib, in which the latter affirms having heard the Prophet say: "In my whole life I have never undertaken anything reprehensible, such as committed by pagans, except for twice, and each time God preserved me from it." And Muhammad recounts how, as a young shepherd, he wanted to have a good time during two soirées of a marriage celebrated in Mecca. But when he arrived at the party, God prevented him from doing what he wanted to do and put him to sleep until the break of day.[1] Here is one of the rare, properly biographical indications that we possess about the first forty years of the life of Muhammad! Moreover, Ibn Hazm reports that in his time it was claimed that "the ban on wine was not part of the *sunna* of the Prophet, and it was something that they

[Muhammad and his companions] would have consumed. May God preserve them from such a thing!"[2]

It is this veritable ideological conditioning founded upon the sacralization of the person of the Prophet that lies at the origin of the Muslim perception of Koranic writing, glorified and made sublime in its turn by an irresistible movement. Thus an insurmountable barrier has been established against any historical and relativized perception of the Koran. Theological reason has triumphed over historical reason. Across the fourteen centuries that separate us from the time of revelation, history has been patiently and methodically rewritten. All the traces that might embarrass the new construction have been gradually eliminated. It is the writings themselves that have most taken the toll for this.

The work was so prompt and has been so thorough that today there remains practically no nonepigraphic writing that dates from the first century of Islam, including the Koran itself. The earliest testimony about the Koran during the first centuries has disappeared in turn forever. As we have just seen, there has also been a scorched-earth policy touching the biography of Muhammad, whether concerning his apostolate or his pagan life. Let us recall here that even the sayings of the Prophet were forbidden to circulate during the first century of Islam. The principal consequence of this *tabula rasa* of the past undertaken by political and religious powers has been to consecrate definitively the new orthodox ideology as the only possible and true one. Henceforth this becomes an ideology that no proof or serious clue can now touch, because any other trace has disappeared—or almost.

The trap has thus enclosed the consciousness of any Muslim. Ideology has taken definitively the upper hand over historical reality, such that it has become perfectly useless to produce any document, to advance any argument, to rediscover any truth about Islam as it actually existed and was lived by Muhammad. One is immediately accused of plotting against Islam, of wanting to do it harm, of deprecating it, and so on. Historical truth has become suspected of impiety, and the falsehood organized by those who hold religious power has proved to be a sure and effective guarantee of the piety of Muslims, who are thereby kept outside of, and in ignorance of, the true theological and historical debates.

The other victim of this ideologically orthodox system is incontestably—and paradoxically—the Koran. Not only were the first Koranic manuscripts destroyed on the caliphs' orders, but the Koran has been emptied of its content, and what has been substituted is a new Koran wholly fabricated from pieces called *sunna,* or a Tradition attributed after the fact to Muhammad. This Tradition is declared "to complete" the Koran, if not to abrogate it, and in any case furnishes us with "correct" explanations that one must adopt, in letter as well as in spirit. Any approach to the Koran necessarily must pass via the traditionalist dogma—otherwise, excommunication. The institution of the *sunna* is a veritable inquisitorial machine of formidable efficacy, so successful has it been in making Muslims believe that it holds a monopoly on truth about divine things, whereas its existence and its content are actually the work of a political system for cornering power. All the evidence shows that the pseudoexegesis of the Koran is just an impressive machine of apologetics that has functioned at the expense of the historical truth about the Koran. The very sacralization of the Koranic text, quite contrary to the Koranic spirit itself, has served as an excellent instrument for stifling definitively the voice of the Koran and its historicity. The historical critique of the Koranic text has by now suffered a lag of a century and a half in relation to the work that has exposed biblical texts to the light of human history.

The Muslim today is ignorant of everything about the Koran, as he is of anything about Muhammad, apart from the mythical clichés that take the place of history. The sacredness with which he surrounds the Koranic text prevents him almost physically from understanding it and discovering that it has meanings that are not those that orthodoxy authorizes, and that there is indeed a history the first Muslims arranged in their fashion that prevents us today from understanding that history—and from better understanding the Koran.

Appendix

THE SOLAR ECLIPSE OF JANUARY 27, 632 CE

THE SOLE SCIENTIFIC DATE

The life of Muhammad is known to us through the Koranic text and various stories reported by Muslim Tradition. But nothing has come down to us to attest with certitude to the veracity of these events, to their exactitude and precise dating. The Koran for its part scarcely gives us any specifics on lived events, leaving open to Muslim chroniclers the most unbridled speculation on the totality (or almost) of facts relating to the life of the Prophet.

By chance, progress in astronomic calculations permits us today, as we shall see, to have for the first time scientific proof about an event that has been reported profusely in Muslim Tradition, but which is not mentioned in the Koran: "the eclipse of the Sun in the time of the Prophet of Allah," as it is devotedly expressed in the *sunna*. Some important events in the life of Muhammad have been associated with this cosmic phenomenon. We now possess even more data about it and therefore the dating of certain surahs of the Koran may be better determined.

Let us try first to show how it is possible for us to determine with certainty which eclipse we are dealing with. For our study, I have drawn on the calculations and advice that Patrick Rocher, astronomer at the Institute of Celestial Mechanics of the Paris Bureau of Longitudes, furnished in the context of my inquiry, for which I thank him here very much.

First, these calculations allow us to say that out of the nineteen eclipses recorded in Mecca and in Medina in Muhammad's lifetime, none offered the total phase that would have produced complete or significant darkness. On the August 2, 612, at a time when Muhammad was beginning his preaching in Mecca, there was an eclipse of the sun that started at 18:48 in the evening (first contact between sun and moon), but thirteen minutes later the sun set, so that the people of Mecca would not have been able to witness the phenomenon, even if the start of the eclipse could have been seen with the naked eye.

Similarly, the following year, on the July 23, 613, Meccans could have observed the most important solar eclipse in the lifetime of the Prophet. It took place at 7:17 in the morning and was over at 9:51, attaining a maximum obscuration of 93.4 percent. Unfortunately, as this maximum was reached about three hours after sunrise, it would have been difficult to observe this eclipse with the naked eye. But the darkness was barely perceptible, for 1 percent of solar illumination is equivalent to that of a hundred thousand moons. We can say the same thing about the three other eclipses of lesser importance visible in Mecca, which occurred on May 21, 616; November 4, 617; and September 2, 620.

After this Meccan period, Muhammad immigrated to Medina in 622, point of departure of the Muslim calendar, that of the Hijra (signifying, we recall, Emigration), more exactly, Friday, July 16 of that year. And the first eclipse of the Muslim era observable in Medina did not take place until two years later, on June 21, 624. But curiously its fate was identical to the first eclipse in Mecca of 612, starting barely a quarter of an hour before the setting of the sun.

The second Medinan eclipse occurred on April 21, 627. It was contemporaneous with the War of the Ditch, in which the Meccans hostile to Muhammad failed in their siege of Medina. But this partial eclipse that happened five hours after sunrise hid only 5.4 percent of the solar disk and hence had very little chance of being observed with the naked eye.

Five years later, or four months and eight days before the death of the Prophet, the third and final Medinan eclipse is undoubtedly the only one it would have been possible to observe unaided, and this one is spoken of in many stories of Tradition. It occurred on Monday, January 27, 632, corresponding to the twenty-eighth of the month of *Chawwâl* of year 10 of the Hijra. The sun began to be eclipsed very early in the morning, at 7:30 min and 19.4 sec, and attained a maximum of 76.6 percent obscuration at 8:45 min and 56.6 sec, and it was entirely gone by 10:13 min and 51.8 sec, or after 2 hours and 43 minutes duration.

We are faced with two eclipses that are very similar: the one on July 23, 613, which started three hours before sunrise, and the one on January 27, 632, starting twenty-one minutes after it. But the stories that have come down to us about Muhammad speak of a single eclipse "in the time of the Messenger of Allah (*fî 'ahd al-rasûl*)." Which eclipse are they talking about, 613 or 632? For as Patrick Rocher has noticed, despite the precocity of the eclipse of 632 (its proximity to the sunrise), it would not have been much more easily observable than the first. The rule has it that observation of the eclipse with the naked eye is only possible during the rising or setting of the sun, not between the two. Taking account of these observations, it remains true that the sun is more easily observable in the presence of clouds or winds of sand when its height is nearer the horizon, which was indeed the case of the eclipse of January 27, 632.

Whatever the case, the literature of the Muslim Tradition, the *hadîths*, gives us a certain number of clues that confirm that the eclipse referred to by the companions of Muhammad is indeed the one we have just identified as the eclipse of January 632. To be exhaustive, let us signal a few contrary indications, notably the one reported by al-Nasâ'î, in his sunan (*Salât al-kusûf*), who has Aïsha say that the eclipse took place during the Meccan period of Muhammad's life, or that it took place in Medina on a very hot day. Could these be confused with events foreign to this context, as is quite often the habit with the literature of the Tradition?

Unfortunately, the stories (with rare exceptions—for example, the one we have just seen regarding the temperature it was on the day of the eclipse) scarcely give any details about it, neither its precise date nor the part of the day when it took place. The only interesting exception is nevertheless important, since it gives us a precise description of the hour it took place. In his sunan, the traditionalist Abû Dâwûd[1] reports a story put into the mouth of a companion of Muhammad named Samurata ibn Jundab, in which he says during a Friday sermon: "While I and a young man of the Allies were shooting arrows [?], the Sun darkened like a *tannûma* [a fruit] at the moment when it was, to the eyes of the observer, at the height of two or three lances from the horizon. We said to ourselves: let us go to the Mosque, for, by Allah, there is going to be something between the Messenger of God and his community as a result of what is happening to the Sun. We rushed there. And then [Muhammad] appeared. He came forward and he proceeded to pray . . ." The Muslim imam, in his *Sahîh*, (*Kitâb al-kusûf*), reports similar stories attributed to the same companion but under the name of Abd al-Rahmân ibn Samurata, and without any of the astronomical details that interest us here.

This testimony from Ibn Samurata on the position of the sun during the eclipse seems to agree with the calculations of the Paris Bureau of Longitudes, which gives a position of the sun at 19 degrees above the horizon at the moment when it reached maximum darkness. Hence this is the sole important clue about this eclipse that we have in all of traditional Muslim literature. Other stories are content to specify that the event took place in the morning, as does Aïsha, the Prophet's wife, who affirms that he observed the eclipse "in the early morning [*ghadât*], while he was astride a mount."[2]

A GREAT ENIGMA

In short, all the scientific data, when correlated with what is transmitted by Tradition, confirm that the only eclipse observable during Muhammad's lifetime and handed down to us took place on the morning of Monday, January 27, 632, at 6:30 AM, Medina local time.

Thus for the first time, an event in the life of Muhammad is proved scientifically with reasonable certainty and dated with never-before-equaled precision. We may even describe the form taken by each phase of the evolving eclipse just as Muhammad and his companions would theoretically have observed it with their own eyes in Medina—at least at the start of the phenomenon. In effect, the movement of the eclipse affected the surface of the sun according to an axis (using a watch face as a guide) of 2 to 8 o'clock, but slightly shifted toward the bottom of the sun, in such a way that the solar crescent pointed obliquely downward and to the right, which was considered by ancient astrology as a rather bad sign.

It was certainly a moment of grand emotion but also of surprise: this eclipse took place four months and one week before the death of the Prophet of Islam. And yet, nowhere in Muslim Tradition is a connection made between this eclipse that so strongly marked the spirit of the young Medina community and the death of Muhammad shortly afterward.

Still, Muslim Tradition has clearly associated an eclipse with the death of Muhammad's son, Ibrâhîm, then a year and a half old, according to some accounts. Sometimes the eclipse has even been dated on the same day as the death of Ibrâhîm. Two traditions, one attributed to the companion Jâbir and the other to Sufyân and Wakî', have them say: "The Sun eclipsed itself in the time of the Prophet, the day when Ibrâhîm, son of the Messenger of Allah, died. So people said: 'The Sun underwent an eclipse for the death of Ibrâhîm.'"[3] Ibrâhîm died at an early age, shortly before Muhammad. This fact confirms the late date of the eclipse. Another event, concerning a conjugal drama, with which we are about to deal, also confirms this late dating of the eclipse to January 632.

However, while Tradition has associated the eclipse with the death of Ibrâhîm, we cannot give the least credence to stories that claim these two events took place on the same day.[4]

In fact, Tradition attributes to Muhammad these words pronounced at the end of the eclipse: "The Sun and the Moon are not eclipsing each other because of the death of someone, nor on the occasion of his birth." This maxim recurs as a leitmotif in most of the stories recording the words of the Prophet during the eclipse. One of the companions of the Prophet, Abû Bikra, comments on this statement in these terms: "And this because a son of the Prophet, called Ibrâhîm, had died and because the faithful made a gloss on it."[5] I share the opinion of Abû Bikra: the death of a young boy must have certainly been on everyone's mind during the eclipse of January 27, 632, but it would be totally mistaken to take this date as that of his death.

Why did Muhammad reject so vociferously any connection between these two events, going so far in a *hadîth* as promising hell for those who said that "The Sun and Moon only go into eclipse for the death of a great man"?[6] It was certainly not because the Prophet did not believe in astrology. Quite the contrary! The Sun and the Moon represent in the Koran important divine "signs" (*âyât*). The *hadîths* even have Muhammad say on the subject of the eclipse: "The Sun and the Moon are indeed two signs of Allah. With their eclipse, God wants to make people afraid. They do not eclipse each other for the death of someone. So if you observe the eclipse, pray and implore Allah until He grants you grace."[7]

This astrotheological incident is important in explaining the fact that no allusion was made in all of Islamic literature to the extraordinary proximity in time between the eclipse and Muhammad's own death. The companions of the Prophet who observed this eclipse and who even prayed with him during this singular and unique event must have been unable, in mentioning it in their reminiscences, to avoid making a connection with his death that occurred only seventeen weeks later. It is quite evidently difficult for them to mention any relation between these two events without committing the sin of affirming, like those who are doomed to hell, that "the Sun was eclipsed for the death of someone human." What is certain is that this eclipse necessarily raised speculation right away within the young Muhammadan community, especially if the death of Ibrâhîm was still fresh in everyone's memory.

The political importance of eclipses to the people of Medina was all the more evident because an immemorial tradition had often associated these astral phenomena with the fate of kings and the outcome of wars. For example, an Assyrian astrological prediction affirms that "if the Sun rises in the form of a crescent and wears a crown like the Moon: [then] the king will take the land of his enemies; evil will quit the land, and the king will be healthy . . ."[8] Muslim Tradition, for its part, associated the eclipse with the end of the world, as reported in a story attributed to the famous companion of the Prophet, Abdallah ibn Mas'ûd: "The Messenger of Allah ordered us to pray during an eclipse of the Sun and Moon: 'If you witness it, take refuge in prayer, for if it is what you fear [i.e., the end of the world] you will not be taken unprepared, and if not, you will have accomplished a good deed.'"[9] Another interpretation advanced was that an eclipse was due to the appearance of Allah before astral bodies that "darkened" out of fear of him.[10]

A CONJUGAL PSYCHODRAMA

The eclipse of January 27, 632, permits us not only to date with better approximation the death of Ibrâhîm, son of Muhammad, but also permits us to date the greatest conjugal drama that the Prophet experienced during the twenty years of his apostolate.

In fact, during the prayers over which the Prophet presided during the eclipse, he had apocalyptic visions, which Ibn Abbâs, the most illustrious of the traditionalists among Muhammad's companions, reports in these terms: "At the end of the prayer, people said: 'O Messenger of God! During your prayer we saw you take something, and then you moved backward.' The Prophet replied: 'I saw Paradise, and there I gathered a bunch of fruit. And if I had truly taken it, you would have eaten some until the end of time. And then I saw the Furnace and never in my life have I seen such a horrible spectacle as that one. And I saw that most of those in it were women.' The people then asked: 'Why, O Messenger of God?' He replied: 'Because of their ingratitude [*kufr*].' They asked him: 'Their ingratitude toward God?' He replied: 'But also toward their companion. They are ungrateful for the good he does for them. Even if you do good for one of these women for an eternity, it suffices for her to get angry just once for her to say to you: "I never saw any good in you"!'."[11]

Ibn Abbâs says not one word here to explain this sudden explosion of misogyny that condemns to hell all of womankind. And for a good reason! It is because Muhammad alludes here in a scarcely veiled way to his own wives, who had just created a resounding scandal when he slept (in the bed of his wife Hafsa, daughter of the future caliph Omar) with her slave Mâriya the Copt. When Hafsa discovered him there, she fulminated against God's chosen one, who quickly recognized his error and promised not to sleep anymore with Mâriya, on condition that she did not spread news of this scandal. But Hafsa could not keep quiet, and soon all the wives of the Prophet were in a rage. Hurt and even wounded by this high treason, Muhammad decided all of a sudden to repudiate all of them and henceforth live with only one woman . . . Mâriya. But after negotiations to find an outcome that might satisfy everyone, the Prophet returned to his wives (having lived effectively one month with his young Coptic slave).

The incident was so serious that the Koran devotes a surah to it; number 66 is called "Prohibition" (*Al-Tahrîm*) and deals with a secret confided to a spouse but soon discovered. Then comes this threat: "If the Prophet divorces you, perhaps his Lord will give him in your place better wives than yourselves, submissive, praying and obedient to Allah, devotees who glorify God, married or virgins" (66:5).

Mâriya the Copt was in fact offered as a present to Muhammad by al-Muqawqis, governor of Alexandria, along with her sister Sîrîn, a mule, an ass, honey, and the ceremonial clothing in which Muhammad was apparently later buried. According to a story told by Ibn al-Athîr, twelfth-century author of the Common Era, the Prophet offered Sîrîn to Hassân ibn Thâbit, his court poet.[12] Ibn al-Athîr states that Mâriya gave birth to Ibrâhîm in the month of Dhû al-Hijja of the eighth year of the Hijra. When the infant was seven days old, they cut and buried his hair according to Arab tradition, and gave him a name. But the wet nurses argued over the baby, states the same author, so as "to free Mâriya for the Prophet, so attached he was to her."[13]

The scandal must have exploded when Ibrâhîm died, shortly before the eclipse. During the prayer of the eclipse on that Monday, January 27, 632, the mosque was still resounding with sarcastic and reproachful remarks addressed to the Prophet over his conduct, as confirmed by a different story attributed to Aïsha, who has Muhammad say during the great day of the eclipse: "O Community of Muhammad! By Allah! Nobody other than Allah cares any longer about preventing his Servant [i.e., Muhammad] or his concubine ['amatuhu, alluding to Mâriya the Copt] from carrying out fornication [yazniya]. O Community of Muhammad! By Allah! If you knew what I know [alluding to his vision during prayers of a hell filled with women], you would have laughed less and cried more."[14]

By all accounts, Tradition tries here—somewhat clumsily, it must be admitted—to exculpate the Prophet. But the choice of the prayer of the eclipse as the context for this explanation could not be due to chance, since evidently this affair was contemporaneous with the cosmic event of the eclipse. It is likely that the death of Ibrâhîm must have been contemporaneous with this conjugal drama, which itself was contemporaneous with surah 66 of the Koran that relates it. And all of this occurred during the days that preceded and followed the eclipse of January 27, 632.

THE ECLIPSE AND THE FAREWELL PILGRIMAGE

Muhammad had probably never observed an eclipse in his life apart from the one that shortly preceded his death. That means the psychological impact and the shock that he felt at the sight of the diurnal star soaring over the Medina sky being amputated of three-quarters of its splendor must have been tremendous indeed. On this point, traditionalist literature is eloquent. A story attributed to Asma, sister of Aïsha, relates that during the eclipse, Muhammad was so seized with panic (*fazi'a*) that he took away a woman's cloak rather than his own.[15] Another story from Abu Mûsâ, a companion of the Prophet, reports that during the eclipse, Muhammad "being seized with panic, rose, fearing the end of the world" and headed for the mosque. At the end of the prayer, he is said to have explained that the eclipse had been "provoked by Allah to cause fear in his Servants. So if you see it again, urgently invoke God, pray to Him and ask Him for pardon."[16]

Did Muhammad think of his own mortality during this long eclipse of almost three agonizing hours that must have seemed an eternity? We saw above his apocalyptic evocations of paradise and of hell during his eclipse prayer. To this should be added a vision of "the torment of the tomb" that awaits those among the dead who respond wrongly to the angels when they ask about the identity of the true Prophet. Aïsha is even reported to have said that, after this vision during the eclipse, the Prophet prayed to God to protect him not only from the torment of hell, but henceforth also from "the torment of the tomb."[17]

It seems, in the light of all these witnesses, that Muhammad was profoundly shaken by the eclipse, and that his infinitely repeated denials of any link between the eclipse and the death of men are formulas designed to exorcize his own death, after the quite recent one of his only son.

How can one otherwise explain the surprising decision that the Prophet of Islam took only a few days after the eclipse: to perform his first pilgrimage to Mecca since he settled in Medina in September 622?

It was now clear to him that the astronomical phenomenon that he observed on that fresh morning of Monday, January 27, 632, was a true "sign from Allah," whose meaning could not escape him. Muhammad arrived in Mecca on March 3 and performed the pilgrimage from March 8 to 10. Then he immediately returned to Medina. Barely three months later, God completed his astral sign: the Prophet died peacefully, close to his favorite wife, Aïsha.[18]

The birth of Ibrâhîm had not been envisaged by Muhammad, since the male infants he had from his first wife, Khadîja, had all died. This is what permits the famous affirmation in the Koran: "Muhammad is the father of no man among you. He is the Messenger of Allah and the Seal of the Prophets" (33:40). It is quite evident that the birth of Ibrâhîm constitutes a refutation of this assertion, which Tradition did not know how to resolve. Al-Râzî posed the question: "The Koran says 'Muhammad is the father of no man among you', and yet he was the father of Tahar, Tayyib, Qâsim and Ibrâhîm." He then replies that all these boys did not reach the age of "manhood."

Some have even envisaged the possibility that this last son would have succeeded Muhammad as *nabî* if he had lived. Baydâwî affirms this in his commentary on the same verse of the Koran: "As the Prophet, may God bless him, said about Ibrâhîm when he died: 'If he had lived, he would have become a *nabî*.'"[19] This is yet another illustration of the fact that the closure of the prophecy by Muhammad is probably only a myth invented by Muslim orthodoxy and was certainly not on the agenda during his lifetime.

Finally, Muslim Tradition has often asserted that the archangel Gabriel came each Ramadan for a session of work with Muhammad to verify and shape the revelations of the preceding year, except for the year of his death, when there were two meetings. Why these two meetings instead of the usual annual one? Tradition has never raised this question. But the answer is obvious: the last Ramadan of Muhammad's lifetime did not coincide with the end of the revelations. Important events like the conjugal drama and especially the farewell pilgrimage gave rise to decisive revelations after the annual rendezvous with Gabriel. Consequently, it was necessary to have a second and final working session. In addition, Tradition has never specified in which month this second exceptional session took place. No doubt people were afraid to engage in more debates over a calendar that was hard to reconcile with the myth of a "collecting" of the Koran effectuated during these so-called celestial annual rendezvous.

NOTES

CHAPTER 1

1. Arthur Jeffery, *The Qur'ân as Scripture* (New York: Books for Libraries, 1980), pp. 202, 205.

2. Ibid., pp. 47–48.

3. Suyûṭî, *Itqân*, I/125, §537.

4. Ibid., I/126, §540.

5. Ibid., I/126, §543.

6. Ibid., I/130, §555.

7. Ibid., I/131, §562.

8. Ibid., I/131, §563.

9. Ibid., I/132, §566.

10. Ibid., I/133, §566.

11. Ibid., I/133, §567.

12. Ibid., I/133, §568.

13. Ibid., I/133, §569.

14. Ibn Mujâhid, *Kitâb al-Sabʿa*, p. 45.

15. Régis Blachère, *Introduction au Coran* (Paris: Maisonneuve et Larose, 1991), 69n89.

16. Ibid., p. 202.

17. Ibn Mujâhid, *Kitâb al-Sabʿa*, p. 106.

18. Blachère, *Introduction au Coran*, p. 203.

19. Ibid., pp. 49–50.

20. Ibn Abî Dâwûd, *Kitâb al-maṣâḥif.*

21. Solange Ory, "Un Nouveau Type de Muṣḥaf," in *Revue des Etudes Islamiques* (1965): 107.

22. Blachère, *Introduction au Coran*, p. 202.

23. Ibid., p. 202.

24. Bokhâri, *Les Traditions*, III/538.

25. *Geschichte des Qorans* I/47.

26. Suyûtî, *Itqân*, I/101, §401.

27. Ibid., §402.

28. Ibid., §403.

29. Ibid., I/102, §405.

30. Ibid., §406.

31. Ibid., §407.

32. Ibid., §408.

33. Ibid., I/102–103, §411.

34. Ibid., §411–15.

35. *Geschichte des Qorans* I/48.

36. Blachère, *Introduction au Coran*, p. 13.

37. Ibn Hanbal, *Musnad*, V/266.

38. Bokhâri, *Les Traditions*, III/520.

39. Suyûtî, *Itqân*, III/66, §4117.

40. Suyûtî, *Itqân*, III/66, §4116.

41. Ibid., §4118.

42. Blachère, *Introduction au Coran*, p. 185.

43. Abî Muhammad al-Qaysî, *Kitâb al-Kashfʿan wujûh al-qirâ'ât al-sabʿ*, éd. crit. Par. M. Ramadhân, 2 vol. (Damascus: 1974), p. 21.

44. De Prémare, *Prophétisme*, p. 108.

45. Ibid., pp. 107–108.

46. Suyûtî, *Itqân*, III/68, §4126.

47. Ibid., §4127.

48. Ibid., §4130.
49. Ibid., III/67, §4122.
50. Ibid., pp. 67–68, §4125.
51. Blachère, *Introduction au Coran*, p. 189.
52. Ibid., p. 190.
53. Régis Blachère, *Le Coran* (Paris: PUF, 1980), 464n13.
54. Ibid., 534n14.
55. Ibid., 500n37.
56. Ibid., 162n91.

CHAPTER 2

1. Régis Blachère, *Introduction au Coran* (Paris: 1959), p. 100.
2. Ibid., p. 173.
3. Ibid., 173n244.
4. Suyûti, *Itqân*, I/182, §870.
5. Ibid., pp. 181–82, §868.
6. Blachère, *Introduction au Coran*, p. 175.
7. Ibid., p. 176.
8. Suyûtî, *Itqân*, I/167, §779.
9. Ibid., §781.
10. Ibid., p. 168, §78.
11. Ibid., §801.
12. Suyûtî, *Itqân*, I/169, §796.
13. Ibid., §797.
14. *Geschichte des Qorans*, I/31.
15. A. T. Welch, *Al-Kur'ân*, in E.I.2 (vol. V), p. 416.
16. Georges Ifrah, *Histoire universelle des chiffres. Lorsque les nombres racontent les hommes* (Paris: Seghers/CNRS, 1981), p. 215.
17. Blachère, *Introduction au Coran*, p. 31.
18. *La Bible. Écrits intertestamentaires* (Paris: Bibliothèque de la Pléiade, 1987), p. 53
19. Ibid., p. 636.
20. Ibid., p. 471.
21. Brigitte Mondrain, "Les Signatures des cahiers dans les manuscrits

grecs," in *Recherches de codicologie comparée. La composition du Codex au Moyen Âge en Orient et en Occident*, ed. Philippe Hoffmann (Paris: ENS, 1998), p. 25.

22. Welch, *Al-Kur'ân*, p. 416.

23. Suyûṭî, *Itqân*, I/167, §781.

24. Régis Blachère, *Le Coran* (Paris: 1980), p. 212.

25. Suyûṭî, *Itqân*, I/179, §852.

26. Blachère, *Le Coran*, p. 666.

27. Suyûṭî, *Itqân*, I/179, §854.

28. Welch, *Al-Kur'ân*, p. 413a.

29. Georges Tartar (Pasteur), "Épître de Abd al-Masîh al-Kindi" in *Dialogue Islamo-Chrétien sous le Calife al-Ma'mûn (813–834). Les épîtres d'al-Hashimî et d'al-Kindî* (Paris: 1985), p. 196.

30. Abî Muhammad al-Qaysî, *Kitâb al-Kashf ʿan wujûh al-qirâ'ât al-sabʿ*, éd. crit. Par. M. Ramadhân, 2 vol. (Damascus: 1974), p. 16.

31. Carra de Vaux, art. "*Basmala,*" *Encyclopédie de l'Islam*, p. 1,117.

32. Al-Qaysî, *Kitâb kashf*, p. 16.

33. Ibid.

34. Suyûṭî, *Itqân*, I/148, §650–736.

35. Ibid., §646–47.

36. Ibid., I/148, §648.

37. Hans-Caspar Graf von Bothmer and Karl-Heinz Ohlig; Gerd-Ruediger Puin: "Neue Wege der Koranforschung," *Magazin Forschung* (Universitaet des Saarlandes, Saarbruecken) 1/1999, Neue Wege: 43–44.

CHAPTER 3

1. Bukhârî, *Fadhâ'il al qur'ân*, bâb 3.

2. Blachère, *Introduction au Coran*, p. 25.

3. Ibid., pp. 22–25.

4. Ibid., pp. 33–34.

5. Ibid., pp. 35–45.

6. Ibid., pp. 46–47.

7. Ibid., p. 54.

8. Ibid., pp. 80–82, 90.

9. Adolf Grohmann, "The Problem of Dating Early Qur'ân in Islam," *Der Islam* 32 (1958): 216.

10. Hans-Caspar Graf von Bothmer and Karl-Heinz Ohlig; Gerd-Ruediger Puin: "Neue Wege der Koranforschung," *Magazin Forschung* (Universitaet des Saarlandes, Saarbruecken) 1/1999, Neue Wege: 41c.

11. Arthur Jeffery, *Materials for the History of the Qur'ân, The Old Codices* (including the Arabic text of Ibn Abî Dâwûd, *Kitâb al-ma*sâhif) (Leiden: 1937), p. 10.

12. Here I am using the pages of the manuscript that have been reproduced on the Web site http://www.callnetuk.com/home/aperfectquran/A1.htm.

13. Mondher Sfar, *Le Coran, la Bible, et l'Orient ancient*, 2nd ed. (Paris: 1998), p. 274.

14. J. Wansbrough, *Quranic Studies: Sources and Methods of Scriptural Interpretation* (Oxford: 1977), pp. 1–12.

15. Ibid., pp. 21–26.

16. Sfar, *Le Coran, la Bible*, pp. 136–46.

17. André Paul, *La Bible* (Paris: 1998), p. 142.

18. Wansbrough, *Quranic Studies*, p. 21.

CHAPTER 4

1. It would be more correct to translate *Fâtiha* by *Incipit,* which is the exact meaning of the word in the minds of the "collectors" of the Koran.

2. I refer the interested reader to the excellent article kindly sent to me by Bord, listed in the bibliography.

3. After the magisterial and rich study by Michael Huber on the legend of the Seven Sleepers, published in 1910, which includes indications on the Arabic literature touching on this theme.

4. In surah 18, *The Cave*, verses 9–26.

5. Isidor Lévy, "Le Chien des sept Dormants," *Annuaire de l'Institut de Philologie et d'Histoire Orientales*, Mélanges Bidez, t. 2/1934, Bruxelles, 581.

6. Jean Lambert, *Le Dieu distribué: une anthropologie comparée des monothéismes*, "Le chien de la caverne endormie et quelques autres récits, aux fondations de la sourate 18," chap. 14 (Paris: 1995), pp. 257–97.

7. Arthur Jeffery, "The Qur'ân as Scripture," *Muslim World*: 189–201.

8. Mondher Sfar, *Le Coran, la Bible, et l'Orient ancient*, 2nd ed. (Paris: 1998), p. 51.

9. See J. Wansbrough, "Revelation and Canon" in *Quranic Studies: Sources and Methods of Scriptural Interpretation* (Oxford: 1977), pp. 1–32.

10. Tabarî, *Annales* I/2952, in Wansbrough, *Quranic Studies*, p. 51.

11. See the excellent examination of this question in an article by Claude Gilliot, "Les 'informateurs' juifs et chrétiens de Muhammad. Reprise d'un problème traité par Aloys Sprenger et Theodor Nöldeke," *Jerusalem Studies in Arabic and Islam* 22 (1998): 84–126.

12. Ibid., p. 88, §9.

13. Ibid., p. 119, §66.

CONCLUSION

1. Ibn Hazm, *Al-Fiṣal fî al-milal wa al-ahwâ' wa al-niḥal*, ed. Abd al-Rahmân Khalîfa (Cairo: 1347 H), IV/25.

2. Ibid., IV/26.

APPENDIX

1. Abû Dâwûd, *Sunan*, vol. I, « *Kitâb ṣalât al-istisqâ'* », hadîth no. 1184.

2. Mâlik, *Muwatta*, vol. I, book 12, hadîth no. 3.

3. Muslim, *Saḥîḥ*, vol. II, book 10 on the eclipse, hadîth nos. 10 and 23.

4. As A. T. Welch seems to do in his article "Muhammad" in the *Encyclopédie de l'Islam*, where he gives the date of June 27, 632, as the day Ibrâhîm died, without mentioning the solar eclipse.

5. Bukhâri, *Saḥîḥ*, "XVI: Des eclipses," hadîth no. 17.

6. Muslim, *Saḥîḥ*, hadîth no. 9.

7. Ibid., hadîth no. 21.

8. F. Richard Stephenson, *Historical Eclipses and Earth's Rotation* (Cambridge: Cambridge University Press, 1997), p. 125.

9. Ibn Hanbal, *Musnad*, I/459.

10. Ibid., IV/267.

11. Mâlik, *Muwatta*, "Kitâb salât al-kusûf," hadîth no. 2.

12. Ibn al-Athîr, *Asad al-Ghâba*, I/38.

13. Ibid., I/39.

14. Mâlik, *Muwatta*, "Kitâb salât al-kusûf," hadîth no. 1.

15. Muslim, *Sahîh*, hadîth no. 14.

16. Ibid., hadîth no. 24.

17. Ibid., hadîth no. 8.

18. It is clear that the Arabs of Hijâz in the time of Muhammad continued to believe in astral signs, although the study of astronomy had made its appearance in neighboring Mesopotamia twenty-two centuries earlier. During the eclipse, Muhammad as a *nabî* (prophet) acted as a veritable diviner, notably in the course of his "prayer," conjuring away the evil fate that was heralded on the face of the sun. The apocalyptic visions that he had were produced while he was in an ecstatic state, when "he started to gasp on the ground and to weep while he was in a posture of prosternation" (Ibn Hanbal, *Musnad*, 2/159). It was at this moment that the Prophet revealed his visions: "Paradise was presented to me, and if I had wanted to, I could have taken some branches from its trees. Then Hell was presented to me, and I blew so as to extinguish it for fear that it would reach you" (ibid.). Other stories specify that during this conjuring prayer, Muhammad "moved backward and the people who were in rows behind him withdrew right to the back of the room. Then he advanced, and the people did likewise" (Muslim, *Sahîh*, *Kitâb al-kusûf*, bab 3, hadîth no. 10). It is clear that what is described here is nothing other than a divinatory ceremony that Tradition has tried to tone down into a ritual prayer. These gestures of advancing and retreating belong to a sun cult known in Carrhae in the north of Syria. This cult "was provided with divinatory rites where the statue of a bearded Appolo rendered oracles by advancing forward to say 'yes' to questions, and withdrawing backward to say 'no'" (Bouché-Leclercq, *Histoire*, III/403–404).

19. Baydâwî, *Anwâr al-tanzîl*, II/130.

BIBLIOGRAPHY

Abd al Azîz al-Rashîd, Sa'd. *Kitâbât Islâmiyya min Makka al-Mukarrama.* Al-Riyâḏ: 1416/1995.

Abd al-Bâqî, Muhammad Fu'âd. *Al Mu'jam al-Mufahras li-alfâdh al-qur'ân al-karîm.* 2nd ed. Beirut, 1991.

Altmann, A. "Saadia's Theory of Revelation: Its Origin and Background." *Saadiya Studies*, Manchester (1943): 4–25.

Augapfel, J. "Das Kitâb im Qur'ân." *Wiener Zeitschrift für die Kunde des Morgenlandes* 29 (1915). 384–93.

Barr, J. *Comparative Philology and the Text of the Old Testament.* Oxford: 1968.

———. *The Semantics of Biblical Language.* Oxford: 1961.

Bayḏâwî. *Anwâr al-tanzîl wa 'asrâr al-ta'wîl.* 2 vols. Leipzig: 1846–48.

La Bible. Écrits intertestamentaires. Paris: Bibliothèque de la Pléiade, 1987.

Bell, R. *Bell's Introduction to the Qur'ân, Completed, Revised and Enlarged by W. Montgommery Watt.* Edinburgh: 1970.

Birkeland, H. *Altarabische Pausalformen.* Oslo: 1940.

Blachère, Régis (trad.). *Le Coran.* Paris: PUF, 1980.

————. *Introduction au Coran*. Paris: Maisonneuve and Larose, 1959.

Blau, J. A. "Grammar of Christian Arabic, Based Mainly on South Palestinian Texts from the First Millennium." *Corpus Scriptorum Christianorum Orientalium Subsidia*, Louvain (1966–67): 27–29.

————. "Some Problems of the Formation of the Old Semitic Languages in the Light of Arabic Dialects." *Proceedings of the Int. Conference on Semitic Studies*, Jerusalem, 1965.

Bloch, A. «Vers und Sprache im Altarabischen.» *Acta Tropica Supplementum* 5. Basel: 1946.

Bord, Lucien-Jean. «'Quand je suis sorti du sein de l'obscurité . . . je t'ai vu.' La poésie sacrée dans le Proche-Orient ancien.» *Conférence* (Spring 1999): 332–70.

————. « Semblances, ressemblances et dissemblances : Le psaume premier et la Fâtiha. » *Cedrus libani* 53: 27–33.

Bothmer, Hans-Caspar Graf von. « Frühislamische Koran-Illuminationen. Meisterwerke aus dem Handschriftenfund der Grossen Moschee in Sanaa/Yemen. » *Kunst und Antiquitäten* (1986), vol. 1.

Bothmer, Hans-Caspar Graf von, Karl-Heinz Ohlig, and Gerd-Ruediger Puin. « Neue Wege der Koranforschung. » *Magazin Forschung* (Universitaet des Saarlandes, Saarbruecken) 1 (1999): 33–46.

Bovon, François. *Révélations et Écritures*. Paris: 1993.

Bräunlich, E. « Versuch einer literargeschichtlichen Betrachtungweise altarabischer Poesien » *Der Islam* 24 (1937): 201–69.

Briquel-Chatonnet, Françoise. « Cahiers et signatures dans les manuscrits de la Bibliothèque Nationale de France » in *Recherches de codicologie comparée. La composition du Codex au Moyen Âge en Orient et en Orient*, ed. Philippe Hoffmann, 153–69. Paris: 1998.

Brockett, Adrien. "The Value of the Hafs and Warsh Transmissions for the Textual History of the Qur'ân" in *Approaches to the History of the Interpretation of the Qur'ân*, ed. Andrew Rippin, 31–45. Oxford: 1988.

Brother Mark, Koranic manuscripts of Samarkand. Online at http://www.call netuk.com/home/aperfectquran/A1.htm.

Burton, John. *The Collection of the Qur'ân*. Cambridge: Cambridge University Press, 1977.

Carra de Vaux, B., art. « Basmala, » *Encyclopédie de l'Islam*², I/1116–17.

Caskel, W. « Ayyâm al Arab : Studien zur altarabischen Epik. » *Islamica* 3 supp. (1931): 1–99.

Caspar, Robert. « Textes de la Tradition musulmane concernant le Taḥrîf (falsification) des Écritures. » *Islamochristiana* 6 (1980): 61–104.

Chapira, B. « Légendes bibliques attribuées à Ka'b al-Aḥbâr. » *Revue d'Etudes Juives* 69 (1919): 70, 86–107; 70 (1920): 37–43.

Corriente, F. "On the Functional Yield of Some Synthetic Devices in Arabic and Semitic Morphology." *Jewish Quarterly Review* 62 (1971): 20–50.

Crone, P., and M. Hinds. *God's Caliph*. Cambridge: Cambridge University Press, 1986.

Culley, R. *Oral Formulaic Language in the Biblical Psalms*. Toronto: University of Toronto Press, 1967.

Daube, D. "Rabbinic Methods of Interpretation and Hellenistic Rhetoric." *Hebrew Union College Annual* 22 (1949): 239–64.

Déroche, François. *The Abbasid Tradition: Qur'ans of the 8th to 10th Centuries. The Nasser D. Khalil Collection of Islamic Art*, vol 1. London/Oxford: 1992.

———. « Les Écritures coraniques anciennes: Bilan et Perspectives. » *Revue des Etudes Islamiques* XLVIII (1980): 207–24.

———. *Les Manuscrits du Coran.* t. I : *Aux origines de la calligraphie coranique*. Paris: 1983; T. II : *Du Maghreb à l'Insulinde*. Paris: 1985.

———. « Les Manuscrits du Coran en Caractères Hijâzî. Position du problème et Eléments préliminaires pour une enquête. » *Quinterni* 1, Fondazione Ferni Noja Noseda, Studi Arabi Islamici. Lesa, 1996.

———. « Les premiers manuscripts. » *Le Monde de la Bible* (Le Coran et la Bible aux sources de l'Islam) 115 (Nov./Dec. 1998): 32–37.

Déroche, François, and Francis Richard, eds. *Scribes et Manuscrits du Moyen-Orient*. Paris: 1997.

Didier, Hugues, « L'Original : Une vaine passion 'Renaissance' » in Hugues Didier, etc., pres., *Les Enjeux de la Traduction. L'expérience des missions chrétiennes. Actes des sessions 1995 et 1996 de l'Association Francophone Œcuménique de Missiologie, et du Centre de Recherches et d'Echanges sur la Diffusion et l'Inculturation du Christianisme*, 147–48. Paris: s.d.

Eickelman, Dale F. "Musaylima. An Approach to the Social Anthropology of Seventh-Century Arabia." *Journal of the Economic and Social History of the Orient* 10 (1967): 17–52.

Elbogen, I. *Der jüdische Gottesdienst in seiner geschichtlichen Entwicklung*. Frankfurt: 1931.

« Épître de Abd al-Masîh al-Kindi. » Pasteur Georges Tartar, *Dialogue Islamo-Chrétien sous le Calife al-Ma'mûn (813–834). Les épîtres d'al-Hashimî et d'al-Kindî.* Paris: 1985, pp. 113–283.

Ess, Josef van. *Theologie und Gesellschaft im 2. Und 3. Jahrhundert Hidschrah. Eine Geschichte des religiösen Denkens im frühen Islam,* I–IV. Berlin/New York: 1991–97.

Fahd, Toufic. Art. « Nubuwwa » in *Encyclopédie de l'Islam.*

———. *La Divination arabe. Etudes religieuses, sociologiques et folkloriques sur le milieu natif de l'Islam.* Thèse Strasbourg: 1966; repr., Paris: Sindbad, 1987.

———. « De l'Oracle à la Prophétie en Arabie. » *Oracles et prophéties dans l'Antiquité, Actes du Colloque de Strasbourg, 15–17 juin 1995,* ed. Jean-Georges Heintz. Paris: 1997.

———. *Le Panthéon de l'Arabie centrale à la veille de l'Hégire.* Paris: 1968.

———. « La visite de Mahomet aux Enfers ; entre la Descente d'Inanna/Ishtar dans le Monde inférieur et l'Enfer de Dante » in T. Fahd, *Etudes d'Histoire et de Civilisation Islamiques,* 225–50. T. II, Les Editions Isis. Istanbul: 1997.

Fischer, W. « Silbenstructur und Vokalismus im Arabischen. » *Zeitschrift der Deutschen Morgenländischen Gesellschaft* 117 (1967): 30–77.

Fück, J. *'Arabiya. Recherches sur l'histoire de la langue et du style arabe,* trad. C. Denizeau. Paris: 1955.

Galliner, S. *Saadia al-fayyûmi's arabische Psalmenübersetzung und Commentar (Psalm 73–89).* Berlin: 1903.

Gerhardsson, B. *Memory and Manuscript: Oral Tradition and Written Transmission in Rabbinic Judaism and Early Christianity.* Copenhagen: 1964.

Gertner, M. "Terms of Scriptural Interpretation: A Study in Hebrew Semantics." *Bulletin of the School of Oriental and African Studies* (1962): 1–27.

Geschichte des Qorans, t. I : Theodor Nöldeke and Friedrich Schwally, *Über den Ursprung des Qor'ans.* Leipzig: 1909; t. II, *Die Sammlung des Qor'ans, mit einem literarhistorischen Anhang über die muhammedanischen Quellen und die neuere christliche Forschung.* Leipzig, 1919; t. III, Gotthelf Bergsträsser and Otto Pretzl, *Die Geschichte des Qorantexts.* Leipzig: 1938.

Gibert, Pierre. *Comment la Bible fut écrite*. Bayard, Paris: 1995.

Gil, Moshe. "The Medinan Opposition to the Prophet." *Jerusalem Studies in Arabic and Islam* 10 (1987): 65–96.

Gilliot, Claude. *Exégèse, langue et théologie en islam. L'exégèse coranique de Tabari*. Paris: 1990.

———. « Les 'informateurs' juifs et chrétiens de Muhammad. Reprise d'un problème traité par Aloys Sprenger et Theodor Nöldeke. » *Jerusalem Studies in Arabic and Islam* 22 (1998): 84–126.

Goldziher, I. « Der khatîb bei den alten Arabern. » *Wiener Zeitschrift für die Kunde des Morgenlandes* 6 (1892): 97–102.

Grami, Amel. *Ḥurryyat al-muʿtaqad fî al-islâm* (The freedom of faith in Islam). Casablanca: Le Fennec, 1997.

———. *Qaḍiyyat al-ridda fî al-fikr al-islâmî* (The question of the apostasy in the Islamic thought). These, Faculté des Lettres de la Manouba. Tunis: 1993.

Grohmann, Adolf. "The Problem of Dating Early Qur'ân in Islam." *Der Islam* 32 (1958): 213–31.

Gruendler, Beatrice. *The Development of the Arabic Script: From the Nabatean Era to the First Islamic Century according to Dated Texts*. Atlanta: 1993. See also F. Scagliarini, in *Orientalia*, Rome, 63 (1994): 294–97.

Haldar, Alfred. *Association of Cult Prophets among the Ancient Semites*. Uppsala, 1945.

Heger, Christoph. *Koranic Manuscripts of San'â*. Online at http://home.t-online.de/home/Christoph.Heger/palimpse.htm.

Heinrichs, W. *Arabische Dichtung und Griechische Poetik*. Beirut: 1969.

Heintz, Jean-Georges. « Alliance humaine—Alliance divine: documents d'époque babylonienne ancienne & Bible hébraïque.—Une esquisse. » *Biblische Notizen*, Munich, 86 (1997): 66–76 (3 tableaux).

———., ed. *Oracles et prophéties dans l'Antiquité, Actes du Colloque de Strasbourg, 15–17 juin 1995*. Paris: 1997.

Heintz, Jean-Georges, and Lison Millot. *Le livre prophétique d'Osée, Texto Bibliographie du XXème siècle*. Wiesbaden: 1999.

Hibatallah. *Kitâb al-nâsikh wa-mansûkh*. Cairo: 1960.

Hirschberg, J. *Jüdische und christliche Lehren im vor und frühislamischen Arabien*. Cracow: 1939.

Huber, Michael. *Die Wanderlegende von des Siebenschläfern. Eine liter-argeschichtliche Untersuchung.* Leipzig: 1910.

Ibn Abî Dâwûd. *Kitâb al-maṣâḥif.* Cf. Jeffery, *Materials for the History of the Qur'ân.*

Ibn Ḥazm, *Al-Fiṣal fî al-milal wa al-ahwâ' wa al-niḥal,* vol. 4, ed. Abd al-Rahmân Khalîfa. Cairo: 1347 H.

Ibn Mujâhid. *Kitâb al-Sabʿa fî al Qira'ât,* ed. Dr. Chawqî Dayf. Cairo: 1972.

Ibn Warraq, ed. *The Origins of the Koran. Classical Essays on Islam's Holy Book.* New York: 1998.

———. *Why I Am Not a Muslim,* foreword by Joseph Hoffmann. Amherst, NY: Prometheus Book, 2003.

Ifrah, Georges. *Histoire universelle des chiffres. Lorsque les nombres racontent les hommes.* Paris: Seghers/CNRS, 1981.

Jeffery, Arthur. *Materials for the History of the Qur'ân. The Old Codices.* Leiden: 1937. (Includes the Arabic text of Ibn Abî Dâwûd, *Kitâb al-maṣâḥif.*)

———. "The Qur'ân as Scripture." *Muslim World* 40 (1950): 41–55, 106–34, 185–206, 257–75.

Jeffery, Arthur, and I. Mendelsohn. "The Orthography of the Samarqand Qur'ân Codex." *Der Islam* (1942).

Johnson, A. « Mashal » *Wisdom in Israel and in the Ancient Near East. Vetus Testamentum,* supp. 3 (1960): 162–69.

Kandil, Lamya. « Die Schwüre in den mekkanischen Suren » in *The Qur'ân as Text,* ed. Stefan Wild, 41–57. Leiden: 1996.

Kelber, Werner. *Tradition orale et Écriture.* Paris: Cerf, 1991.

Koch, Klaus. *The Growth of the Biblical Tradition.* London: Scribner, 1969.

Künstlinger, D. « Sab'an min al-mathânî. » *Orientalistische Literaturzeitung* (1937): 596–98.

Lambert, Jean. *Le Dieu distribué: une anthropologie comparée des monothéismes,* foreword by P. Geoltrain. Paris: 1995.

Lévy, Isidor. « Le Chien des Sept Dormants. » *Annuaire de l'Institut de Philologie et d'Histoire Orientales.* Mélanges Bidez, t. 2 (1934): 579–84.

Loewe, R. "The 'Plain' Meaning of Scripture in Early Jewish Exegesis." *Papers of the Institute of Jewish Studies,* Jerusalem (1965): 140–85.

Lüling, G. *Über den Ur-Qoran. Ansätze zur Rekonstruktion der vorislamisch-christlichen Strophenlieder im Koran.* Erlangen: 1974, 1993.

Margoliouth, D. "The Origins of Arabic Poetry." *Journal of the Royal Asiatic Society* (1925): 417–49.

Maṣāḥif Ṣanʿâ, exhibition catalog, March 19–May 19, 1985, Kuwait National Museum of Art: Hussa Sabah Salîm al-Sabâh, G. R. Puin, M. Jenkins, U. Dreibholtz (in Arabic and French).

Mehren, A. von. *Die Rhetorik der Araber*. Copenhagen–Vienna: 1853.

Mingana, A. "Syriac Influence on the Style of Kur'an." *Bulletin of the John Rylands Library*, Manchester (1927).

Mondrain, Brigitte. « Les Signatures des cahiers dans les manuscrits grecs » in *Recherches de codicologie comparée. La composition du Codex au Moyen Âge en Orient et en Orient*, ed. Philippe Hoffmann, 21–48. Paris: 1998.

Monnot, Guy. « Le corpus coranique » in *La Formation des canons scriptuaires*, ed. Michel Tardieu, 61–73. Paris: Cerf, 1993.

Monroe, J. "Oral Composition in Pre-Islamic Poetry." *Journal of Arabic Literature* 3 (1972): 1–53.

Muilenburg, J. A. "Study in Hebrew Rhetoric: Repetition and Style," supp. *Vetus Testamentum* (1953): 97–111.

Müller, D. H. *Die Propheten in ihrer ursprunglichen Form: die Grundgesetze der Ursemitischen Poesie erschlosse und nachgewiesen in Biebel, Keilinschriften, und Koran*. Vienna: 1896.

Müller, F. *Untersuchungen zur Reimprosa im Koran*. Bonn: 1969.

Nadîm, al-. *Kitâb al fahrast*. Beirut: 1988.

Nöldeke, Theodor. *Geschichte des Qorans*. Göttingen: 1860.

Obermann, J. "Islamic Origins: A Study in Background and Foundation" in *The Arab Heritage*, ed. Nabih Amin Faris, 58–120. Princeton, NJ: 1944.

Ory, Solange. « Un nouveau type de mushaf. Inventaire des Corans en rouleaux de provenance damascaine, conservés à Istanbul. » *Revue des Etudes Islamiques* (1965): 87–149.

Paul, André. *La Bible*. Paris: 1998.

Pedersen, J. "The Islamic Preacher : wâ'iz, mudhakkir, qâss," in *Goldziher Memoria*, 226–51. Vol. 1. Budapest: 1948.

Penrice, John A. *Dictionary and Glossary of the Koran*. Delhi: 1990.

Prémare, Alfred-Louis de. « Les éléphants de Qâdisiyya » in *Arabica* 45 (1998): 261–69.

———. « L'histoire du Coran comme document écrit » in *Le Monde de la*

Bible, « Le Coran et la Bible aux sources de l'Islam » 115 (Nov./Dec. 1998): 25–31.

———. « Prophétisme et adultère, d'un texte à l'autre, » *Revue du mondes musulmans et de la Méditerranée* (Les premières écritures islamiques) 58 (1991): 101–35.

Puin, Gerd-Ruediger. "Observations on Early Qur'an Manuscripts in San'a'" in *The Qur'an As Text*, ed. Stefan Wild, 107–11. Leiden/New York/Cologne: E. J. Brill, 1996.

Qattân, Mannâʿ al-. *Fî ʿulûm al qur'ân*. Cairo: 1997.

Qaysî, Abî Muhammad al-. *Kitâb al-Kashfʿan wujûh al-qirâ'ât al-sabʿ*, ed. M. Ramadhân. 2 vols. Damascus: 1974.

Qur'anic Studies on the Eve of the 21st Century: A Symposium. June 10–12, 1998, Leiden University, Leiden.

Rabin, C. *Ancient West-Arabian*. London: 1951.

———. *Qumran Studies*. Oxford: 1957.

Rossi, Pierre. *La Cité d'Isis. Histoire vraie des Arabes*. Paris: 1976.

Saadya. *Kitâb al-amânât wal-iʿtiqâdât*. Leiden: 1880.

Schapiro, I. *Die haggadischen Elemente im erzählenden Teil des Korans*. Leipzig: 1907.

Schwarzbaum, H. "The Jewish and Moslem Versions of Some Theodicy Legends." *Fabula* 3 (1959–60): 119–69.

Seeligmann, I. « Voraussetzungen der Midraschexegese. » Supp. *Vetus Testamentum* 1 (1953): 150–81.

Sfar, Mondher. *Le Coran, la Bible et l'Orient ancien*. 2nd ed. Paris: Sfar, 1998.

Sidersky, D. *Les Origines des légendes musulmanes dans le Coran*. Paris: 1933.

Sister, M. « Metaphern und Vergleiche im Koran. » *Mitteilungen des Seminars für Orientalische Sprachen* 34 (1931): 104–54.

Speyer, H. *Die Biblischen Erzählungen im Qor'ân*. Hildesheim: 1961.

Steinschneider, M. *Polemische und apologetische Literatur in arabischer Sprache*. Leipzig: 1877.

Stephenson, F. Richard. *Historical Eclipses and Earth's Rotation*. Cambridge: Cambridge University Press, 1997.

Stetter, E. *Topoi und Schemata im ḥadîth*. Tübingen, 1965.

Strack, H. *Introduction to the Talmud and Midrash*. Philadelphia, 1945.

Suyûṭî. *Al-Itqân fî'ulûm al-qur'ân*, ed. Saïd al-Mundarawh. 4 vols. Beirut: 1996.

Ullmann, M. *Untersuchungen zur Ragazpoesie*. Wiesbaden: 1966.

UNESCO Web site. Uzbekistan, Holy Koran Mushaf of Othman. Online at http://www.unesco.org/webworld/nominations/en/uzbekistan/reading.htm.

Vermes, G. *Scripture and Tradition in Judaism*. Leiden: 1961.

Veyne, Paul. *Comment on écrit l'histoire*. Paris: Seuil, 1971.

Vollers, K. « Arabisch und Semitisch: Gedanken über eine Revision der semitischen Lautgesetze. » *Zeitschrift für Assyriologie* 9 (1894): 165–217.

———. *Volkssprache und Schriftsprache im alten Arabien*. Strasbourg: 1905.

Wansbrough, J. *Quranic Studies, Sources and Methods of Scriptural Interpretation*. Oxford, 1977.

———. *The Sectarian Milieu. Content and Composition of Islamic Salvation History*. Oxford: 1978.

Welch, A. T. « Al-Kur'ân » *Encyclopédie de l'Islam*, t. V.

Wellhausen, J. *Reste arabischen Heidentums*. Berlin: 1927.

Westermann, C. *Grundformen prophetischer Rede*. München: 1968.

Wieder, N. *The Judean Scrolls and Karaïsm*. London: East and West Library, 1962.

Yousif, Ephrem-Isa. *Les philosophes et les traducteurs syriaques. D'Athènes à Baghdad*. Paris: 1997.

Zwettler, M. *The Oral Tradition of Classical Arabic Poetry*. Columbus, OH: Ohio State University Press, 1978.

Zunz, L. *Die Gottesdienstlichen Vorträge des Juden*. Frankfurt: 1892.

INDEX

'Abasa surah 80, 63. *See also* Koranic texts for specific verse citations

Abdallah ibn Mas'ûd. *See* Ibn Mas'ûd, Abdallah

Abd al-Malîk (caliph), 75, 76, 79

Abd al-Rahmân ibn 'Awf, 38

Abraham, 33, 37, 42, 47, 55, 71, 102

abrogation, 10, 30, 32, 37, 82, 95, 97, 104

Abû al-Aswad al-Du'ali, 75

Abû Ayyûb, 33

Abû Bakr (caliph), 10, 24, 65, 70, 71, 72, 73, 74, 75, 78, 94

Abû Bikra, 110

Abû Dâwûd, 108

Abû Hayyân, 77

Abû Mûsa al-Ash'ari, 38–39, 73, 114

act of inspiration. *See wahy* [act of inspiration]

Adam, 84

adultery, 53–54, 102

Aïsha, 32, 37, 53–54, 108, 109, 113, 114

al-Ahzâb [Confederate Tribes] surah 33, 37. *See also* Koranic texts for specific verse citations

'Alam nashrah surah 94, 63. *See also* Koranic texts for specific verse citations

al-an'âm ["Herd"] surah 6, 64.

See also Koranic texts for specific
   verse citations
al-'anfâl surah 8, 62. *See also*
   Koranic texts for specific verse
   citations
al-A'raf ["The Heights"] surah 7,
   62. *See also* Koranic texts for
   specific verse citations
Al-Asr ["The Declining Day"] surah
   103, 23, 24. *See also* Koranic
   texts for specific verse citations
al-Aswad al-'Anasî, 66
al-Baqara ["The Heifer"] surah 2,
   37, 79. *See also* Koranic texts
   for specific verse citations
al-Dhuhâ surah 93, 63. *See also*
   Koranic texts for specific verse
   citations
al-Falaq surah 113, 39. *See also*
   Koranic texts for specific verse
   citations
al-Fîl surah 105, 62. *See also*
   Koranic texts for specific verse
   citations
al-Hafd ["The Race"] (prayer), 39
al-Hajjâj (governor), 11, 75, 76, 79
Alî (caliph), 23, 73, 74, 78
Ali ibn Abî Tâlib, 102
Al-i-Imran ["The Family of
   Imran"] surah 3, 57. *See also*
   Koranic texts for specific verse
   citations
Al-Juwaynî, 20
al-Khal' ["The Denial"] (prayer), 39
Al-Kindî, 65
al-Kutba, 82

Allah, 101–102, 113
   allowing modification of Koran,
      26–28
   creating the Koran, 15, 46, 50
   forgiving and punishing, 47, 48
   guiding Muhammand on way to
      communicate, 32, 70
   and his Apostle, 25, 26, 33–34,
      35, 50. *See also* Muhammad
   Merciful Benefactor, 39, 62, 64
   Messenger of Allah, 33, 44, 107,
      108, 110, 111, 115. *See also*
      Muhammad
   mysterious letters glorifying
      Allah, 54–61
   Prophet of, 35, 50, 105. *See also*
      Muhammad
   replaced in Samarkand manu-
      script, 80
   and Satan, 10, 28–30, 31, 44
   signs of, 45–46, 50, 110, 111, 114,
      115
   speaking to Moses, 42, 45
   See also al-Rahmân; God
A.L.M., 54–55, 56, 57, 67
al-Marwâ, 41
A.L.M.R., 55, 67
A.L.M.S., 67
al-Muqawqis (governor), 113
al-Nasâ'î, 108
al-Nûr ["The Light"] surah 24,
   53–54, 55. *See also* Koranic
   texts for specific verse citations
al-Qaysî, 66
al-qurâ'n. See qur'ân [recitation]
A.L.R., 57

al-Rahmân, 64–67
  use of the term in the Koran, 64
al-Râzî, 21, 62, 115
Al-Tahrîm ["Prohibition"] surah 66,
  112. *See also* Koranic texts for
  specific verse citations
al-Tawba ["Repentance"] surah 9,
  37, 62, 63, 64. *See also Barâ'a*
  ["Innocence"] surah 9; Koranic
  texts for specific verse citations
alterations, God preserving Koran
  from, 16, 101
  conflict with need to change over
    time, 27
al-wâqi'a ["The Event"] surah 56,
  63. *See also* Koranic texts for
  specific verse citations
ambiguity, 29–30
  ambiguous revelations, 30
  and mode of revelation, 31–34
  theory of ambiguous verses, 97
Anas ibn Mâlik, 22, 32–33, 35, 38,
  68
An-Nas surah 114, 39. *See also*
  Koranic texts for specific verse
  citations
apocalyptic visions of Muhammad,
  112, 114
Apocrypha, 71
apologetics, 88, 92, 104
apostolate of Muhammad, 47, 51,
  84, 88, 91, 99, 102, 103, 111
Arabic language
  difficulties of writing Arabic,
    71–72, 75–77, 95
  Koran revealed in, 19–20

perfect Arabic-ness of the language of the Koran, 88
Asma, 113
assonance as a criteria for division
  of Koran into verses, 50
astrology, 110–11
authenticity of Koranic text, 9–10,
  16, 22
  as authentically divine, 94
  authenticity of *wahy*, 98–100
  complexity of questioning, 101
  inauthenticity, 19
  literal authenticity of, 87, 90–93,
    98
  myth of authenticity, 81–82
  preambles acting as certificates
    of, 55
  of prophetic apostolate, 99
âya [sign], 26, 27, 42, 45, 46, 83
  and astrology, 110–11
  explicit *âya* [*bayyinât*], 53
  as a textual division in the Koran,
    50, 52
  use of the term in the Koran, 50

Barâ'a ["Innocence"] surah 9, 37,
  52, 63. *See also al-Tawba*
  ["Repentance"] surah 9;
  Koranic texts for specific verse
  citations
Baruch (scribe), 83
basmala [liturgical formula], 37, 62,
  63–64
  and *al-Rahmân*, 64–67
  legal opinions on, 66
Basra, 73

Bassora, 75
Bay<u>d</u>âwî, 115
bayyinât [explicit *âya*], 53
believers, testing faith of, 28
Bell, R., 58
Bergsträsser, Gotthelf, 11
Bible, 35, 68, 102
    censured by Muslims, 88
    New Testament, 85
    parallels with Koran, 88–89
Biblical texts
    Ezekiel 13:3, 6, 29
    Habakkuk 2:1–2, 83
    Jeremiah 36:1–4, 83
    John 21:25, 35
    1 Kings 22:21–22, 29
    Psalms 1, 89–90
Bibliothèque Nationale de Paris,
    49–50, 76
bi'r ma'ûna, battle of, 38
blacksmiths, 98–99
Blanchère, Régis, 11, 39, 43–46, 50,
    62, 72, 75
blasphemy, 9
Book of Blessings, 59–60
Book of Jubilees, 60
Book on the Seven Readings [*Kitâb
    al-sab'a fî al qira'ât*] (Ibn
    Mujâhid), 22, 95
Bord, Lucien-Jean, 89
Bothmer, Hans-Caspar Graf von,
    68, 76
Bultmann, Rudolf, 12

cadence, 99
Cairo edition of the Koran, 50–51, 62

canon, Koranic, 65, 94
    fixing the Koranic canon, 37
    See also noncanonic Koran
celestial tablet, 10, 15–22, 26, 30,
    83
    leading to revealed text, 54–55,
    56, 87, 90–93
    See also kitâb
certificates of authenticity, 55
chapters of the Koran. *See* surahs
Christianity, 31, 35, 60
classification of verses, 58
clear revelations [*mu<u>h</u>kam*], 29–30
codicological practice, 59, 60, 68
collecting the Koran into a struc-
    tured book, 10–11, 60–61,
    69–86, 87, 94–95, 116
companions of the Prophet, 22, 32,
    73–74, 78, 108, 112, 114
compilations, revelations in the
    form of, 71
compiling the Koran. *See* collecting
    the Koran into a structured book
composition of the Koran, 77
Confederate Tribes. *See* al-A<u>h</u>zâb
    [Confederate Tribes] surah 33
conformance of the Koran to the
    heavenly original, 10, 15–22,
    30, 54–55, 56, 83, 87, 90–93
conjugal psychodrama, 111–13
contradictions in the Koran, 97
conventions and respectability, 25

<u>d</u>alla [straying], 90
Damascus, 73
dârash [to seek], 84–85

dating of events via solar eclipse, 105–16
Dawood, N. J., 89
Day of Last Judgment, 63, 89
death associated with an eclipse, 109–11, 114
declension, 21
"Denial, The." *See al-Khal‹* ["The Denial"] (prayer)
derogation of the Koran, 48
descent. *See tanzâl* [descent]
destruction of Koranic manuscripts, 96, 104
devils. *See shayâṯîn* [devils]
dhikr, 16–17
diacritical signs, 21, 58, 75–76, 95
dispensation, 47–48
Ditch, War of the, 107
divergences in the Koran, 22, 23, 39–40, 51, 74, 95
divine editing, 10
divine inspiration, 20, 91–92, 97
divine laws, mankind obeying, 37
divine preservation of the Koran, 87, 96
divine revelation, 29, 34, 70
division of the surahs, 62–64, 79
divorce, 112
djinns, 28, 97
dogmas, 9, 36, 44, 87, 96, 100, 104
duplications in Koran, 43, 61

eclipse of the sun, 105–16
elaboration of the Koran, 19, 28, 34, 52, 58, 59, 67, 77, 83, 92, 93, 98, 99

emigration to Medina, 34, 46, 47, 106
Encyclopdeia of Islam, The (Welch), 58
end of the world, 111
Enoch, 60
Erra (god), 92
"Erra/Nergal" (poem), 92
erroneous interpolation, 44
Essene writings, 59–60
Eve, 84
"Event, The." *See al-wâqi‹a* ["The Event"] surah 56
"Exordium." See Fâtiha ["Opening, The," "Exordium"] surah 1
Ezekiel 13:3, 6, 29

fables, 98
faith of believers, testing, 28
fallibility of Muhammad, 44
falsehood, test of, 29
false prophet, 29, 65, 70. *See also* Musaylima al-Hanafî
false revelations, 10, 28–30, 31, 86
"Family of Imran, The." *See Al-i-Imran* ["The Family of Imran"] surah 3
faraẓnâha [sanctioning] of surahs, 53–54
fâṣila [break], 50
father of no man, 115
Fâtiha ["Opening, The," "Exordium"] surah 1, 22–23, 34, 39, 74, 78, 89, 90. *See also* Koranic texts for specific verse citations

fawâtîḥ, 54–61
fiqh [theory of justice], 36–37
first form. *See raṭb* [first form]
fixed revelations. *See thabbata*
   [fixed revelations]
Flügel, Gustav, 51
forgetfulness, 32, 44
Formgeschichte, 12
fragmentation of text, 60–61
fragments of text found, 68
French National Library. *See* Bibliothèque Nationale de Paris
funerary lamentations. *See qayn/*
   qayna [funerary lamentations]

Gabriel (archangel), 11, 15, 19–20,
   81–82, 83, 92, 97, 115
   setting the order of the verses, 52
Gahanna, 47
Geschichte des Qorans [*History of
   the Koran, The*] (Nöldeke), 11
Gilliot, Claude, 98–99
God, 9, 10, 19, 24, 36, 48, 60, 90,
   97, 101–102
   allowing modification or suppres-
     sion of parts of the Koran, 26,
     30, 31, 37, 82, 91
   alternate names for, 64–65
   and the celestial tablets [*kitâb*],
     15, 16, 17, 20, 29–30, 81, 96,
     97
   fear of, 20, 110
   having right of abrogation of
     Koran, 82
   keeping Muhammad from evil,
     102–103, 114

omnipotence of, 28, 34, 41, 42,
   56, 63, 98
omniscience of, 34, 57, 98
ordering Satanic revelations,
   28–30
power of, 42, 43, 45, 56, 102
prayers and praise, 39, 56, 57, 89
preserving the Koran from alteration, 16, 17–18, 26, 35, 95, 96
punishment and forgiveness of,
   38, 64, 90, 114
and Satan, 10, 28–30, 31, 44
as source of the Koran, 10, 15, 16,
   17, 19, 20, 38, 53, 77, 83, 97
   See also Allah; *al-Raḥmân*; *rabb*
   [Lord]
Gospels, 19
graphics and letters, 21
great enigma, 109–11
Great Mosque of Sanaa, 76
Grohmann, Adolf, 76

Habakkuk 2:1–2, 83
Hadad (god of thunder), 65
hadîth, 20–21, 32–33, 85, 96, 108,
   110
Hafsa, 72, 73, 112
haggadah, 84, 85
halakah, 85
Hammurabi, 83
Ḥamza, 66
Hârut (angel), 40
Hassan, 102
Hassân ibn Thâbit, 47, 113
heavenly tablet, 94. *See* celestial
   tablet

Hebrew language, 50
"Hedjazian" writing, 76
"Heifer, The." *See al-Baqara* ["The
Heifer"] surah 2
"Hejazian," 49–50
"Herd." *See al-anʿâm* ["Herd"]
surah 6
history of the Koran, 9–12
History of the Koran, The
[*Geschichte des Qorans*]
(Nöldeke), 11
H.M., 55
H̱.M., 56–57, 61
H.M. ʿS.Q., 56
hudûd [limits], 45

Ibn Abbâs, 39, 50, 112
Ibn Abî Dâwûd, 77
Ibn al-Arabî, 50–51
Ibn al-Athîr, 113
Ibn ʿAmir, 46
Ibn Âmir al-Yaẖsubî, 77
Ibn Ashta Abî al-Iṣfahânî, 77
Ibn Hanbal, 21, 96
Ibn H̱azm, 102–103
Ibn Kathîr, 46
Ibn Masʿûd, Abdallah, 21–22, 23,
24, 25, 26, 39, 74, 78, 111
Ibn Mujâhid, 22, 23, 32, 95
Ibn Qutayba, 21
Ibn Samurata, Abd al-Rahmân, 108
Ibn Shanabûdh, 77
Ibn Umm ʿAbd', 24–26
Ibn Warraq, 12
Ibrâhîm (son of Muhammad),
109–10, 111, 113, 115

Idris, 55
Ifrah, Georges, 59
ikhtilâfât [divergences], 95, 97
ʿilm [legal prescriptions], 35
immutable original, 18
inauthenticity, 19
incipit of surahs, 37, 54–61
incoherences in Muslim doctrine, 11
incompleteness of revelations, 35
inferior revelations, 30
infidels, 48
"informants," 98
inimitability of the Koran, 65, 87,
96–97
"Innocence." *See Barâ'a* ["Innocence"] surah 9
inspiration, act of. *See waẖy* [act of
inspiration]
inspirational, divine, 20, 91–92, 97
inspiration and scribes, 82, 92
Institute of Celestial Mechanics,
Paris Bureau of Longitudes,
106
interpolation of the revealed text,
40–48, 49
erroneous interpolation, 44
Introduction au Coran (Blachère),
11
introductions to chapters of the
Koran. *See* preambles
inversion of terms in the Koran, 22
Ishum (god), 92
Ismael, 55
ʿIṣmat ibn Mâlik, 96
isolated letters. *See* mysterious letters
Itqân (Suyûṭî), 32

Jâbir, 109
jam', 94–95
Jeffery, Arthur, 91
Jeremiah 36:1–4, 83
Jesus, 19, 25, 36, 41, 55
Jews and Jewish traditions, 12, 19, 71
John 21:25, 35
Jones, Alan, 58
Judaism, 31, 35
jurists opinions on basmala, 66
justice, theory of. See fiqh [theory of justice]

Kaaba, 45
Kabbalah, 84
Kabti-ilâni-Marduk, 92
kâhins [soothsayers], 97
Khadîja, 115
Khâlid ibn al-Walîd, 65
1 Kings 22:21–22, 29
kitâb, 16, 81
  God guarding, 27
  preservation of, 17–18
  relationship of revealed text to, 17, 35, 81
  sent by God, 9, 10, 15, 16, 17, 20, 29–30, 81
  See also celestial tablet
Kitâb al-kashf (al-Qaysî), 66
Kitâb al-kusûf, 108
Kitâb al-sab'a fî al qira'ât [Book on the Seven Readings] (Ibn Mujâhid), 22, 95
Koran
  Cairo edition of, 50–51

compiling the Koran, 10–11, 60–61, 69–86, 87, 94–95, 116
conformance to the heavenly original, 15–22, 30, 54–55, 56, 83, 87, 90–93
destruction of Koranic manuscripts, 96, 104
divergences in, 22, 23, 39–40, 51, 74, 95
duplications in, 43, 61
elaboration of, 19, 28, 34, 52, 58, 59, 67, 83, 92, 93, 98, 99
fixing the Koranic canon, 37, 65
fragments of text, 24, 60–61
inimitability of, 65, 87, 96–97
Koranic manuscripts destroyed, 104
leather-covered Koran not burning, 96
noncanonic Koran, 38–39, 78
number of surahs in, 78
number of verses in, 50–51, 66
parallels with other religious works, 88–90
preambles, 54–57, 62, 64, 69
preservation of, 87, 95–96
recension of, 61, 73, 75, 78
rectification of, 77
redaction of, 21, 45, 59, 69–86
removal of two prayers from Koran, 39–40
repetition within, 45, 93
sheets of, 60–61, 70, 71, 72, 94
style as a criteria for division into verses, 94
variants of, 22–26

vulgate, 23, 24, 25, 51, 61, 62, 63, 66, 74, 78, 80.

See also qur'ân [recitation]; revealed text; surahs; verses in the Koran

Koranic commentaries. *See tafsîr*

Koranic texts

1:6, 22–23

2:1–2, 55

2:20, 21

2:62, 41

2:89, 19

2:98, 33

2:102, 40

2:106, 27, 32, 82

2:108, 27

2:125, 33

2:153–162, 41

2:177, 45

2:187, 45–46

2:189, 42

2:237, 24

2:255, 57

2:282, 51

2:283, 80

2:284, 80

3:1–2, 57

3:7, 30

3:18, 45

3:28, 48

3:37, 80

3:78, 80

3:87–88, 48

3:89, 48

3:92, 41

3:113, 80

3:144, 33

3:146–47, 80

3:164, 50

4:97, 34, 47

4:98, 34, 47

4:99, 34

4:164, 42

5:3, 35

5:46, 19

5:48, 19

5:67, 31

5:69, 41

5:109, 41

5:119, 80

6:25, 42

6:73, 51

6:91, 46, 71, 80

6:92, 63, 64

6:93, 31

6:112, 28

6:128, 80

7:1–2, 55

7:25, 80

7:85–93, 84

7:157, 45

9:64, 52

9:128–29, 52

10:1, 55

10:15, 31

10:82, 24

11:5, 51

11:5–7, 51

11:9–10, 51

11:12, 31, 55

11:44, 43

11:45–47, 43

11:84–95, 84
12:1–2, 55
13:1, 55
13:38, 27, 28
13:38–39, 26
13:39, 30
14:1, 55
14:24–27, 90
15:9, 16
15:87, 70
16:14, 43
16:101–102, 27
16:103, 98
17:73–75, 31
17:88, 96
17:110, 65
18:27, 18
18:109, 35
19:2, 55
19:64–65, 55–56, 62
20:1–4, 56
20:51–52, 17
22:52, 28–30
22:52–53, 29
23:12, 33
23:14, 33
24:1, 53
24:2–10, 54
24:11–26, 53–54
24:16, 33
24:27–28, 48
24:29, 48
24:33, 48
24:60, 43
25:4–5, 93, 98
25:63, 43
26:1–2, 55

26:176–90, 84
26:196, 89
26:224–28, 47
27:1, 55
27:11, 44
27:19, 44
28:1–2, 55
28:62, 43
28:74, 43
29:18–23, 42
31:1–2, 55
31:27, 35
32:1–4, 56
32:23, 42
33:20, 25
33:40, 115
34:12, 97
35:12, 43
35:31, 18
36:35–36, 51
39:1, 57
40:23, 50
40:35, 45
41:1–3, 55
42:1–2, 57
42:52, 91
43:1–4, 55
43:2–4, 18
43:3, 19
44:1–4, 56
44:7, 56
44:43–44, 22
45:1–2, 57
46:1–2, 57
46:15, 43–44
47:20, 52
48:17, 43

52:21, 47
53:36, 71
55:7–9, 42
56:78–79, 17
57:13, 21
57:17, 41
58:4, 25
60:4, 47
61:6, 25
65:11, 26
66:5, 33, 112–13
70:4, 41
73:6, 22
75:16–19, 32
80:13–15, 82
80:13–16, 17, 71
85:21–22, 17
87:19, 71
89:1, 51
98:3, 71
101:5, 25
103:1–3, 23
103:3, 63
104:8, 25
112:3, 22
Kûfa, 73
"Kufic Koran of Samarkand." *See*
    Samarkand (Kufic manuscript)

language of the Koran, 88. *See also*
    Arabic language
lawh, 15
leather-covered Koran, 96
legal prescriptions. *See ʿilm* [legal
    prescriptions]
legal texts, 37
Legend of the Seven Sleepers, 90

letters
    and graphics, 21
    mysterious letters, 10, 54–61, 67,
        69, 74
    Tradition of the Seven Letters,
        20–21
    use of in the preambles, 54
Lévy, Isidore, 90
"Light, The." *See al-Nûr* ["The
    Light"] surah 24
limits. *See hudûd* [limits]
literal authenticity, 87, 90–93, 98
literal nature of revelations, 83–84,
    87, 90–93
liturgical formula. *See basmala*
    [liturgical formula]
Lord. *See rabb* [Lord]
lost texts, 36–39
Loth, Professor, 58

Mahabharata, 90
mahfûz, 17
maktûb, 17
manipulation
    of the revelation, 31, 34
    from variation to manipulation,
        26–28
Mâriya the Copt, 112, 113
Mârut (angel), 40
Mary (mother of Jesus), 55
Maryam surah 19, 55–56, 62, 64.
    See also Koranic texts for spe-
    cific verse citations
masâhif, 37
mathânî, 70–71, 85
mawwâl, 99
meaning, transmission of, 18–20

Mecca, 34, 73, 102
    converted of, 47
    as "mother of cities," 18
    Muhammad preaching in, 106
    Muhammad's final pilgrimage to,
        35, 115, 116
    solar eclipses in, 107, 108
    stations on the way to, 41
    the taking of in 630, 46
Medina, 34, 54, 62
    emigration to, 34, 46, 47, 106
    siege of, 107
    solar eclipses in, 106–107, 108,
        109
memorization of the Koran, 95–96
Messenger of Allah, 33, 44, 107,
        108, 110, 111, 115. See also
        Muhammad
metallurgical skills, 98–99
Micaiah, 29
midrash, 84
Miqdâd ibn ʿAmr, 73
misinterpretation of the Koran, 21
misogyny, 112
modes
    of revelation, 31–34
    of transmission, 19–20
    of variation, 21
modification of the Koran, 26–28,
        30
Mosaic law, 91
Moses, 24, 27, 42, 44, 55, 71
    God speaking to, 42, 45
"Mother of the Book" [umm al-
    kitâb], 18, 26–28, 30
mouth of God, 85

Muhammad
    apocalyptic visions of, 112, 114
    apostolate of, 88, 99, 102, 111
    collecting the Koran attributed to,
        87
    commenting on recitation of
        Koran, 24
    death of, 10, 11, 35, 40, 50, 99,
        107, 109, 111, 115
    fallibility of, 44
    final pilgrimage to Mecca, 35,
        115, 116
    forgetfulness of, 32, 44
    inspired spirit, 91
    life of, 102–103, 105–16
    meetings with archangel Gabriel,
        11, 81, 83, 97, 115
    Messenger of Allah, 33, 107, 110,
        111, 115
    orders not to change the revealed
        text, 17–18
    pilgrimage to Mecca, 35, 115, 116
    Prophet of Allah, 35, 105
    receiving the revealed texts, 19,
        70, 89
    sacralization of, 103
    setting the order of the verses,
        51–52
    and solar eclipse, 105–16
muhkam [clear revelations], 29–30,
        85
Musʿab ibn ʿUmayr, 33
musaddiq, 18, 19, 85
Musaylima al-Hanafî, 65–66, 70, 71
Mushaf, 94
musical genre, 99

Muslim Tradition, 9–12, 32, 34, 57, 66, 73, 74, 85, 86, 88, 92, 96, 97, 98, 102, 104, 105, 107, 109, 111, 113, 115–16
Muslim World, The (journal), 12
mutashâbih [ambiguous verses], 97
mysterious letters, 10, 54–61, 69, 74
  functioning as titles, 67
myths
  of authenticity, 81–82
  of collection, 94–95, 116
  created by Muslim Tradition, 12
  of inimitability, 96–97
  mythical reconstructions, 87
  of originality, 87, 88–90
  of perfect transmission, 95–96
  of Uthmân, 78–79

nabî, 115
Nabû, 82
"Names of surahs" (Suyûtî), 68
naskh [abrogation], 95
New Testament, 85
Nicholas II (czar), 79
Ningirsu (god), 83
Noah, 43
Nöldeke, Theodor, 11, 58
noncanonic Koran, 38–39, 78
notebooks, signature of, 60

omnipotence, divine, 28, 41, 42, 56, 63, 98
omniscience, divine, 34, 57, 98
"Opening, The," see Fâtiha
  ["Opening, The," "Exordium"]
  surah 1

Oqba ibn ʿÂmir, 73
order of verses, 49
originality, myth of, 87, 88–90
Ory, Solange, 24

Pândavas, 90
panic and solar eclipse, 114
Paris Bureau of Longitudes, Institute of Celestial Mechanics, 106, 108
pen of the Prophet, 85
People of the Book, 26
Pharaoh, 24, 44
phraseology and stereotypes, 83–84
Pickthall, Marmaduke, 51
pilgrimage to Mecca
  Muhammad's final pilgrimage to Mecca, 35, 115, 116
  stations on the way, 41
Pissarev, Dr., 79
prayers, removal of two from Koran, 39–40
preambles, 54–57, 62, 64, 69
precedence of immutable original, 18
preservation
  of the *kitâb*, 17–18
  of the Koran, 87, 95–96
"Prohibition." *See Al-Tahrîm* ["Prohibition"] surah 66
pronunciation, 21
Prophet of Allah, 35, 105
prophets, idealization of, 102
psalm. *See zabûr* [psalm]
Psalms 1, 89–90

Qâsim (son of Muhammad), 115
qayn/qayna [funerary lamentations], 98–99
qirâ'ât [readings], 95
Qumrân, 60
qur'ân [recitation], 17, 61, 70, 83, 93, 94, 96
  al-qur'ân, 85–86
  derived from *kitâb*, 16, 17, 19, 54, 56, 81, 87, 90–93
  people of knowledge, 55
  See also Koran; revealed text
"Qur'ân as Scripture, The" (Jeffrey), 12
Quranic Studies (Wansbrough), 12
Qurayshites, 65, 82, 86
Quraysh surah 106, 62. *See also* Koranic texts for specific verse citations

rabb [Lord], 64
"Race, The." *See al-Hafd* ["The Race"] (prayer)
Rahmân, 65
Ramadan, 81, 115
ratb [first form], 24–26
readings. *See qirâ'ât* [readings]
recension of the Koran, 61, 73, 75, 78
recitation, 55. *See qur'ân* [recitation]
recomposition, textual, 40, 84–85
rectification of the Koran, 77
redaction of the Koran, 21, 45, 69–86
  and mysterious letters, 59

removal of two prayers from Koran, 39–40
"Repentance." *See al-Tawba* ["Repentance"] surah 9
repetition within the Koran, 45, 93
respectability and conventions, 25
revealed text, 16
  archangel Gabriel meeting with Muhammad, 11, 81, 83, 97, 115
  completeness of, 34–36
  drawn from a *kitâb*, 17, 54–55, 56
  gathering into a single volume, 10–11, 60–61, 69–86, 87, 94–95, 116
  God allowing himself to suppress a portion of, 30
  importance of term *âya*, 50
  interpolation of, 40–48
  as a secondary document, 10, 15–22
  two versions of, 24
  See also Koran; *qur'ân* [recitation]
revelations, 31, 52, 70, 71, 92
  ambiguous revelations, 30
  authenticity of, 98
  and *âya*, 50
  clear revelations [*muhkam*], 29–30
  divine revelation, 29, 34, 70
  false revelations, 10, 28–30, 31, 86
  fixed revelations [*thabbata*], 30
  as grace, not as a work of art, 36–39
  incompleteness of, 35

inferior revelations, 30
literal nature of, 83–84, 87, 90–93
manipulation of, 31, 34
mode of revelation, 31–34
revealed themes, 71
Satanic revelations, 28–30
suppressed revelations, 30
textual composition, 72
transmission of, 20–22, 32, 92
whole revelation, 34–36
revisions of Koran, 25
reworking of Koran, 24–26
rhetorical conventions, 83–84
rhyme
    as a criteria for division of Koran
        into verses, 50, 51
    and mysterious letters, 61
    and structure of the Koran, 93
rhythm, 51, 99
Rocher, Patrick, 106, 107

Sa'd Ibn Mu'âdh, 33
sab'ahruf, 20
sab'qirâ'ât, 20
sacralization
    of the Koran, 104
    of Muhammad, 103
saddaqa, 18
Safâ, 41
Sahîh, 108
St. Petersburg, 79
Salât al-kusûf (al-Nasâ'î), 108
Sâlim ibn Ma'qil, 73
Samarkand (Kufic manuscript), 64,
    79–81
Samurata ibn Jundab, 108

sanctioning [faraznâha] of surahs,
    53–54
Satanic revelations, 10, 28–30, 31,
    44
sawâb, 21
scandals and Muhammad, 111–13
Schwally, Friedrich, 11, 58
scientific dating of solar eclipse,
    105–16
scribes and Koran, 85–86
    dishonesty causing curse on them,
        92
    fallibility of, 96
    "informants," 98–99
    scribes shaping the text, 92–93
    trustworthiness of oral and written
        transmission, 87
    writing as scribal function, 82–83
secretaries. See dârash [to seek];
    scribes and Koran
sentence structure, 21
Seven Readings, 20–21, 80
Seven Sleepers, 90
Shamash (god), 83
shayâtîn [devils], 28
sheets of the Koran, 60–61, 70, 71,
    72, 94
Shu'ayb, 84
sign. See âya [sign]
signature of the notebooks, 60
sirât, 23
Sîrîn, 113
solar eclipse, 105–16
Solomon (king), 40–41, 44, 97
sons, death of Muhammad's sons,
    109–10, 111, 113, 115

soothsayers. *See kâhins* [sooth-
    sayers]
"stars of Heaven," 102
stereotypes and phraseology, 83–84
straying. *See ḏalla* [straying]
style as a criteria for division of
    Koran into verses, 50
stylization of the Koran, 77
substitution of words in Koran,
    22–23
Sufyân, 109
suḥufs [sheets of the Koran], 71, 94
Sumeria, 17
sunna, 104, 105
suppressed revelations, 30
surahs, 10
    ʿ*Abasa* surah 80, 63
    al-Aḥzâb [Confederate Tribes]
        surah 33, 37
    ʿ*Alam nashraḥ* surah 94, 63
    al-anʿâm ["Herd"] surah 6, 64
    al-ʿanfâl surah 8, 62
    al-Aʾraf ["The Heights"] surah 7,
        62
    Al-Asr ["The Declining Day"]
        surah 103, 23, 24, 63
    al-Baqara ["The Heifer"] surah 2,
        37, 41, 79
    al-Dhuḥâ surah 93, 63
    al-Falaq surah 113, 39
    al-Fîl surah 105, 62
    al-Ḥijr surah 15, 37
    Al-i-Imran ["The Family of
        Imran"] surah 3, 57
    al-Nûr ["The Light"] surah 24,
        37, 53–54, 55

Al-Taḥrîm ["Prohibition"] surah
    66, 112
al-Tawba ["Repentance"]/*Barâʿa*
    ["Innocence"] surah 9, 37, 52,
    62, 63
al-wâqiʿa ["The Event"] surah 56,
    63
An-Nas surah 114, 39
    arbitrary composition of, 40
    barâʿa surah 9, 52
    dating of, 106
    division of, 62–64, 79
    as editorial units, 53
    Fâtiha ["Opening, The,"
        "Exordium"] surah 1, 22–23,
        39, 51, 74, 78, 89, 90
    incipit of surahs, 54–61
    inequality of length of, 79, 94
    longest, 79
    Maryam surah 19, 55–56, 62, 64
    number of in Koran, 78
    Quraysh surah 106, 62
    sanctioning of, 53–54
    titles of, 67–68
    use of the term in the Koran,
        52–54
    See also Koran; Koranic texts for
        specific verse citations
Suyûtî, 19, 21, 32, 33–34, 37,
    51–52, 67–68
synonyms, 21
Syriac language, 59, 93

Tabarânî, 96, 98
Tabari, 22
tablet. *See* celestial tablet

tafsîr, 85
Taher (son of Muhammad), 115
tanzâl [descent], 91
tasdîq, 85
Tashkent, 79
Tayyib (son of Muhammad), 115
testing
  faith of believers, 28
  zeal of mankind for obeying
    divine laws, 37
test of falsehood, 29
textual recomposition, 40
T.H., 56
thabbata [fixed revelations], 30
thematic unity, 40
themes, revealed, 71
Thôt, 82
titles of surahs, 67–68
Torah, 19, 25, 89
Tradition of the Seven Letters,
  20–21
transcription of the Koran, 96
transmission
  of meaning, 18–20
  modes of transmission, 19–20
  myth of perfect transmission, 87,
    95–96
  of revelations by Muhammad, 32,
    92
  of variants, 20–22
trustworthiness of oral and written
  transmission, 87
Truth, 18, 20, 24, 27, 55, 56, 57
T.S., 55
T.S.M., 55, 57
Tulayhâ al-Asadî, 66

Ubayd Allah ibn Ziyâd, 75
Ubayy ibn Ka'b, 21, 23, 25–26, 39,
  46, 61, 62, 73, 74, 78
Uhud, battle of, 33, 80
Umar (caliph), 21, 24, 32–33, 38,
  52, 62, 70, 72, 73
umm al-kitâb "Mother of the Book,"
  18, 26–28, 30
umm al-qurä, 18
unambiguous text, 30
univocal notations, 58
unretained texts, 36–39
Urukagina, 82
Uthmân (caliph), 10, 20, 37, 39,
  51–52, 62, 73, 74–75, 94, 96
  myth of, 78–79
"Uthmânian" recension, 75, 77, 78.
  See also vulgate

variability of texts as a blessing, 22
variants
  of the Koran, 22–26
  theory of, 20–22
  from variation to manipulation,
    26–28
verb tenses, 21
Verse of the Throne, 57
verses in the Koran
  and *âya*, 50
  classification of, 58
  number of verses in Koran,
    50–51, 66
  oft-repeated verses, 70–71
  order of verses, 51–52
  as the textual unit, 49–52
  See also Koran; Koranic texts for

specific verse citations

vulgate, 23, 24, 25, 51, 61, 62, 63, 66, 74, 78, 80. *See also* Koran

wahy [act of inspiration], 81, 83, 91, 97

authenticity of, 98–100

Wakî, 109

Walîd I, 76, 79

Wansbrough, John, 12, 83–84

War of the Ditch, 107

Welch, A. T., 58, 61

whole revelation, 34–36

women, Muhammad's views about, 112–13

word variations, 21

writing as scribal function, 82–83

trustworthiness of oral and written transmission, 87

See also scribes and Koran

Yamâna, battle of, 70

zabûr [psalm], 89

Zachariah, 55

Zayd ibn Hâritha, 33

Zayd ibn Thâbit, 34, 59, 70, 78, 93, 94

zirât, 23